How to
OVERCOME

HOW TO
OVERCOME

A Practical Exposition
Of Romans 12:14–21

JAY E. ADAMS

P&R
P U B L I S H I N G
P.O. BOX 817 • PHILLIPSBURG • NEW JERSEY 08865-0817

Unless otherwise indicated, Scripture quotations are from
the *NEW AMERICAN STANDARD BIBLE*®. ©Copyright
The Lockman Foundation 1960, 1962, 1963, 1968, 1971,
1972, 1973, 1975, 1977. Used by permission.

Italics within Scripture quotations indicate emphasis added.

Printed in the United States of America

**The Library of Congress has cataloged the first edition
as follows:**

Adams, Jay Edward.
    How to overcome evil.

    Includes bibliographical references.
        1. Christian life—1960—   . 2. Good and evil.
I. Title.   II. Title: Evil.
BV4501.2A285   1977   248.4   83-3280
ISBN-10: 0-87552-022-7 (pbk.)
ISBN-13: 978-0-87552-022-3 (pbk.)

ISBN: 978-1-59638-222-0

Contents

Preface   7

Introduction   9

1. Are You a Winner?   13

2. You Can Be a Winner   17

3. The Evil You Fight   23

4. You Are in a War   27

5. Battle Orders for Today   33

6. Is Aggression Christian?   39

7. The Weapons of Your Warfare   43

8. Your Mouth Is a Problem   51

9. How to Manage Your Mouth   61

10. You Can't Fight Alone   71

11. You Are Part of God's Army   79

12. No Exceptions Allowed   89

13. Plan with Finesse   99

14. Make War, Make Peace   105

15. Three Ways to Be a Troublemaker   115

16. Christian Vigilantes?   123

17. Make Room for God!   135

18. Meet Your Enemy's Need   141

19. Pour on the Coals   147

20. Epilog   151

Preface

I HAVE NOT PREVIOUSLY discussed this extremely important issue in any of my writings. It is new territory. However, the following material, consisting largely of a practical exposition of the latter portion of Romans 12, is not new to our counseling practice. The sort of biblical instruction given in this book has been used over the years to help many persons who find themselves in hand-to-hand combat with evil.

It is my hope that this book will find widespread usage among Christians in general and particularly will be used as assigned reading for counselees who are struggling with the problems to which it is addressed. I believe that counselors everywhere will find it to be an important adjunct to their counseling ministry. I have kept it small and brief for this reason.

Because so many Christians are defeated precisely at the point of their response to attacks on them by evil persons, and because I know of no handbook written in simple style, yet faithful to the

Scriptures, to which they can be directed for guidance and strength, I hope that in some measure by the publication of this book to meet that need. The book is concerned not only with *what* a Christian must do to overcome evil but—like the passage on which it is based—*how* to do so.

Jay E. Adams, 1977
Dean of the Institute of Pastoral Studies
The Christian Counseling & Educational
Foundation

Introduction

"HE CAN'T DO THAT to me! I'll fix him; I know just how to get even. First I'll. . . ." Such words not infrequently fall from the lips of Christians, and not only from those who are immature and disobedient. Any Christian who reads his Bible knows that they are wrong. But how many—even among the more mature Christians—know what to do about the attitudes behind those words? How many know what the Christian attitude should be? And how do you develop it?

When somebody wrongs me, should I retaliate in any way at all? Am I to be totally passive? Is that what turning the other cheek means? How do I handle my feelings if I am hurt or angry? And, what about my immediate reactions? Sometimes I lash out and fight back (at least with words) before I have even had time to think about what I am doing. I seem to be a creature of habit, and my habits are so hard to break. I have good intentions of doing otherwise, but my practice so often fails to measure up to them. I'm defeated more often than not in my battle with evil. Isn't there some way that I can learn at least to stand my ground? Or, am I doomed for the rest of my earthly life to failure? I try to control my tongue but it isn't easy. And, even when I don't say the wrong things I know what I am thinking . . . and I know that isn't right. But one of my biggest problems is to know what is right. Where can I find that out, and when I do, will I be able to do it? That's my problem in a nutshell. Are you puzzled by such questions?

It is possible, of course, that you have discovered God's answers to these questions and that you are successfully following them in your everyday activities. You have learned how to respond properly to your unsaved mother-in-law when she criticizes your cooking or tells a friend that you weren't good enough to marry her son. It may be that you no longer have trouble handling your attitudes toward the boss when he fails to recognize your extra efforts and instead finds fault with you and blames you for what others have done. Once you didn't say much about it (you couldn't afford to lose your job) but you certainly thought all sorts of hard things against him. And at times—unthinkable as it may seem—you have caught yourself pray-ing (praying, I said) that God would remove him from his job, or even once or twice that He would remove him from the earth. More than once you have said (under your breath) "damn him." And you knew these subvocal thoughts and words were wrong and regretted it. Perhaps, in the very midst of this struggle, you have discovered God's answer, and through repentance and the prayerful application of the Bible to your work situation you have found the way to overcome these sins. The Holy Spirit has not only changed you by removing these attitudes, but He has helped you to replace them with biblical thoughts and words that have made you the victor over evil. In fact, your changed attitudes have brought about new conditions that have led to several recent opportunities to witness to your boss.

If you are winning the battle with evil, then you probably don't need this book. You are one of the few who, in our time, is able to grapple successfully with the enemy. Thank God, keep up the struggle, and show others how to do so too.

But perhaps you are like so many—defeated, dismal, and despairing. You have tried and tried and failed and failed. And perhaps you have concluded, "I'm just not the apostle Paul. He could win the war with evil and say he had fought the good fight successfully; I can't and I haven't and I don't see how I ever will." If that's how it is with you, then my friend, this book is for you. You have the same resources to draw on that Paul had. God hasn't changed. Your problem may be that you have tried the wrong things, or tried the right things wrongly. But there is a right way, and a right way to walk in it. Take heart! Cheer up! God hasn't failed you. Read and do what follows and—like many others who have discovered God's way and how to walk in it—you too can overcome evil.

CHAPTER 1

Are You a Winner?

"A WINNER? Me, a winner? You've gotta be kidding? I'm a born loser. I couldn't win a game of checkers against a blindfolded opponent with two hands tied behind his back if I started with a board full of kings! That's rich, think of it! Me a winner! Ha!"

But you can be, in spite of what you have just said. Indeed, if you have trusted Jesus Christ as your Savior, you have no other option. He says you *may* be a winner, insists that you *must* be a winner, and (indeed) *commands* you to be a winner. You have no choice.

Let me assure you at the outset, however, that you will never become a winner so long as you continue to tell yourself that it is impossible. We use language for two purposes: to talk to others and *to talk to ourselves*. We may not convince others too often, but when we talk to ourselves

we are usually most persuasive! People who say
such non-Christian things as "I'm a born loser"
first convince themselves that it is true, then live
like it. It is a sin for Christians to use language
so loosely. The fact is that if you have been born
again, you are literally a born winner! Christ
calls Christians "overcomers" (lit. "winners") and
then tells them: "He who overcomes, I will grant
to him to sit down with Me on My throne, as
I also overcame, and sat down with My Father
on His throne" (Rev. 3:21 NASV). Indeed, you
have been "born again to a living hope . . . an
imperishable and undefiled inheritance [that
won't] fade away [and is] reserved in heaven for
you who are protected by the power of God"
(1 Peter 1:3–5 NASV). That is the description
of a born *winner!* Get rid of such sinful clichés;
let's think scripturally together for a while and
you may see things quite differently a lot sooner
than you think.

To begin with, let's try to understand something about a number of Paul's letters. Frequently,
Paul divides his letters into two main parts: a
doctrinal section followed by a practical one.
In the book of Ephesians, for example, the first
three chapters deal with God's eternal, sovereign
plan of salvation. Then, in the last three chapters,

Paul takes up the practical implications of what he has just said for Christian living. In effect, he says, "On the basis of these great truths let me tell you how to walk as a Christian." The two sections are not separate but are hinged together with a "therefore."

The same is true of the book of Romans. Chapters 1–11 deal with man's sin, God's salvation, the sanctification of the believer, and the calling of the gentiles into God's covenant community. Then, in chapter 12, Paul says, "I urge you therefore brethren, by the mercies of God (i.e., "I base this appeal on the grace of God in saving you as I have shown in the previous section of my letter") to present your bodies a living and holy sacrifice." As they previously had presented the members of their bodies to sin to serve sin's purposes (6:13, 19), now, having been saved by God's mercy, they were to present their bodies for God's righteous service. The rest of chapter 12 and the chapters that follow explain how this may be done in actual day-by-day living.

In chapter 12, Paul stresses the need for making a sober evaluation and a proper use of the Holy Spirit's differing gifts to honor God and bless His church; then, the chapter concludes with these words:

Bless those who persecute you; bless and curse not.

Rejoice with those who rejoice, and weep with those who weep.

Be of the same mind toward one another; do not be haughty in mind, but associate with the lowly. Do not be wise in your own estimation.

Never pay back evil for evil to anyone. Respect what is right in the sight of all men.

If possible, so far as it depends on you, be at peace with all men.

Never take your own revenge, beloved, but leave room for the wrath of God for it is written "Vengeance is Mine, I will repay, says the Lord.

But if your enemy is hungry, feed him, and if he is thirsty, give him a drink; for in so doing you will heap burning coals upon his head."

Do not be overcome by evil, but overcome evil with good. (Rom. 12:14–21, NASV)

We will be studying these verses in depth, because in them lie the answers to most of the questions that can be asked about overcoming evil. I hope that when we are through, its principles will be etched into your thinking and your daily living will be thoroughly marinated in them.

CHAPTER 2

You Can Be a Winner

"WELL, I'M WILLING to hear you, but you're going to have to do some pretty fancy footwork to convince me because I've had my hopes up any number of times before only to have them come crashing down around my feet. That hurts, and I don't want to be hurt again. So go ahead, but remember, I'm going to be cautious and I'm going to evaluate everything you have to say very closely because I've had it with all those pious platitudes that don't work."

Fine, that's all I ask of you. But open to the Scriptures and their specific application to your problems and you will discover solutions that you may not have dreamt of before.

We're going to begin with verse 21: "Do not be overcome with evil, but overcome evil with good." Although it is the final verse in the section, and even though we must go back and work through the previous verses, it is well to begin here because in this verse we have the grand conclusion toward which all the other verses move. Here is the challenge and the hope. Because of this verse we know that victory over evil is a genuine possibility.

In these words there is nothing of the attitude of many modern Christians who think, "If I can hang in by my toenails when the going gets tough that's more than I could hope for." Instead of victory thinking, this eleventh-hour mentality reasons, "I just hope I don't lose too much ground," and, "I hope I can keep my nose above water." Such attitudes are akin to the spirit of the third servant in Matthew 25 who said, "See you have what is yours" (v. 25). His idea was, "If I can only hold on to what my lord gave me that will be success." But his lord thought differently and called him a "wicked lazy servant." He was expected not merely to preserve something but to make a profit. God won't settle for maintenance thinking; He wants to see positive advance, growth. The battle is an *opportunity* and not merely a challenge for you to advance in your Christian life. That is one reason God sends evil your way.

Yet, Christians with a defeatist mentality expect to go down in flames. Theirs is a mentality that is calculated to lose. Because they have the idea that they *won't* win they *don't* win. You rarely find what you are not looking for.

You are not to sink beneath the waters of evil; you are not to bail out when the flak gets thick. You are to win. Wherever the battle breaks out, it isn't the Christian but the forces of evil that should limp from the field crippled by defeat: "Do not be overcome by evil, but overcome evil with good." God has provided both the plan and the power for doing so. The biblical mentality, then, is, "Come on men, we can beat the enemy with God's resources. Let's go after him!"

We'll be talking about how to overcome evil. It isn't enough to *say* "do it"; we must show *how* it can be done. But before turning to the ways and means, we must lay some groundwork and get a clear picture, along with some enthusiasm and vision for it.

If there is anything that counselors find again and again, it is defeated and overwhelmed people who believe that their situation is hopeless because of the evil that others have done to them. Over and over they hear, "So and so did this to me; my parents did it to me. My wife/husband did it to me. My boss did it to me. Circumstances did it to me." Now, of course, these persons may have wronged you—in any number of vicious ways.

We won't dispute that. Evil is all too prevalent in this world; we need not question that point. But suppose they did do something to you? Suppose, for that matter, that they wronged you severely. So what? Is that reason for defeat?

No one should be surprised when he is mal-treated in a world of sin; that's only to be expected. Apart from Christ, there is no perfect person. "All have sinned" (Rom. 3:23). If that is so, it should not be a surprise that others have wronged you, even wives, husbands, parents, and children. Both believers and unbelievers will wrong you—often with evil intent. So, does that excuse you? Does that allow you to sit there defeated, helplessly licking your wounds, blaming someone else for your dilemma? No. How do I know that? Because Christ commands you, "Do not be overcome by evil." By that command, He (1) acknowledges the certainty that you must grapple with wrongdoing directed toward you, (2) holds you responsible for successfully withstanding the attack, and, (3) indeed, insists that you must overcome the wicked one. Those words hardly sound like there is any place for self-pity or excuses. Surely they allow no place for defeatism. In this verse, then, Jesus Christ says, "Do not be overcome by the wrongs that others do to you." That is one of the first things you must see as you begin this study. A Christian can never rightly say, "There was nothing I could do; he attacked me and won." He has been obligated by his Commander in Chief not to lose the battle. The enemy must not be allowed to win.

Now, defeated Christians (and there are far too many of them) think that their situation is beyond hope, that the wrongs done against them are too tough to handle, and so they make excuses for defeat. Not only does this command bring with it the conviction that any such attitude is sin, but it also provides hope. The great General never commands His troops to do anything that they cannot do. If they follow His orders, rely on the power of His Spirit, and follow His example, they can fulfill every requirement that He has laid on them. Excuses, in the Lord's army, are never acceptable.

At first such commands may seem difficult. The demand always to resist and defeat the enemy is stringent and seems only to bring conviction of personal failure and sin. But when the Christian recognizes the fact that every command and requirement of Christ reflects a genuine possibility, since He knows our limitations and our strength, and He in His sovereign wisdom sends nothing our

way that we can't handle (if we handle it His way).[1]
This further reflection on the situation brings hope.
And that hope, in turn, leads to the perseverance
that is needed to endure trials and win battles (cf.
1 Thess. 1:3, where Paul writes about "the perseverance that comes from hope").

So then the command, "Do not be overcome
by evil, but overcome evil with good," is a clear
witness to the fact that you *can* be a winner in the
battle against evil. No matter where or when it
occurs, regardless of its impact or force, there is no
attack that can be made that you cannot withstand
if you do so by using God's weapons, according to
God's revealed strategy, and are energized by His
powerful Spirit. There is hope in that. You are a
born—born-again—winner, so you can start winning those battles *today!*

---

1. Cf. especially my *Christ and Your Problems* (Presbyterian &
Reformed Publishing Co.), a booklet in which this theme is fully
developed from 1 Cor. 10:13.

CHAPTER 3

The Evil You Fight

WHAT IS THIS EVIL that Christ commands you to resist and overcome? Whenever you are engaged in warfare, you must understand your enemy. Otherwise, you will lose the battle.

The evil in view in Romans 12 is not some general evil that happens to exist in the world. It is not abstract. As I have already assumed in the two earlier chapters, it is evil oriented toward *you!* It is suffering that you must endure that is inflicted by some other person. It is motivated—as all wrongdoing is—by the evil one whose intention is to thwart God's purposes by tempting you to sin. He wants to defeat you to bring disgrace on God's name and to weaken His cause. When you are defeated, therefore, it is more than a personal tragedy. Christ's church suffers and His name is slandered. Your Savior has commanded resistance and victory for His own name's sake! Here is your highest motivation of all—you must be a winner to honor Him and strengthen His church.

The essence of this evil, then, lies not in the fact that it has power to cause suffering (that is its effect) nor in the fact that it was unprovoked (that makes it heinous), but most of all in the fact that it is aimed at God. Evil, as it is contemplated in this chapter, is evil against a Christian because he is a Christian. That the perpetrator of the evil doesn't recognize the motive behind his action or the ultimate object of his attack makes no difference. The soldiers in an army rarely understand the ultimate strategies behind the battles that their leaders command them to fight. That the devil's servants (or God's servants temporarily "used" by the enemy) act against God when they do evil to another is a fact, whether it is understood by them or not. The *fact* is not altered by ignorance or protest to the contrary.

This evil, as I have just intimated, may come through a sinning believer, but in this chapter it is wrongdoing inflicted by an unbeliever that is mainly in view. However, what is said about responding to the evil actions of an unbeliever can, with some important qualifications, also be said about responding to a believer. At appropriate points I intend to mention some of these qualifications as we progress.

So this chapter speaks of evil attacks on you, not evil out there that you watch from a distance like you watch a TV show. It is evil that involves you, evil you can't sidestep, evil that demands a response.

Through no fault of your own, evil is directed toward you because as a believer you have been living a life that contrasts with sin. (We are not here dealing with punishment merited by a sinning Christian. As Peter puts it, "By no means let any of you suffer as a murderer, or thief, or evildoer, or a troublesome meddler, but if anyone suffers as a Christian . . ." 1 Peter 4:15, 16).[1] Christ was put to death because of His righteous life. He was the Light of the World. Because His life beamed so brightly they wanted to extinguish it. The contrast with the darkness of men's lives was too great to bear. Either sin and darkness had to go or the Light had to be extinguished. They hated the Light and wouldn't come to Him because He exposed their own deeds as evil. So they tried to put it out. John says that even though they tried to put out the Light they could not *overcome* it. Rather, the Light overcame them (John 1:5).

Light always wins. Shadows can't drive light away; it is light that makes the shadows of darkness

---

1. This passage occurs in a context quite similar to Rom. 12. Cf. 1 Peter 4:14.

disappear. When the sun rises, the darkness has no power against it. The Sun of Righteousness has risen. Its beams have been shining and the darkness is in rout. Because of this, you can defeat the enemy.

The power of the Light of life is in you, Christian. The Sun has made you a light—i.e., a winner in the battle with darkness! You will be hated by the forces of darkness, and they will try to extinguish your light. But you can—you must—overcome. You are light. Light overcomes darkness; darkness can't overcome light. Take that to heart, and go forth to victory!

Remember, then, this evil is undeserved wrongdoing, It is directed primarily not at you but at the Light. I am not talking about such things as your hurt pride because others failed to recognize you as you might have liked to be recognized, or about retaliation for some wrong first done by you, or someone's response to your sinful living, snobbishness, or foolish witnessing tactics. This evil comes because your life is a rebuke to sin, and the sinner doesn't like it.

CHAPTER 4

You Are in a War

"THE EVIL I *FIGHT*?" you ask. Yes, the evil you must fight. "Does God really want me to fight? I know you've been using military language so far, but is it really warranted? I thought that a Christian was to turn the other cheek. That doesn't sound like fighting back. What are you talking about, anyway?" We'll take one thing at a time. And we'll cover all these questions before we are through. But for now, notice one thing: you are in a war.

The word "overcome" ("Do not be *overcome* by evil, but *overcome* evil with good") is a war word. It comes right off the battlefield with the smell of smoke and sweat still clinging to it. The term is used to describe a defeat; to be overcome is to be defeated in battle. To overcome, on the other hand, is to defeat the enemy. You are in the battle of your life. Your battle is with sin wherever it is found—within you, outside you. Here, of course,

Paul is thinking of those sinful attempts that others make to hurt you. Through them Satan wants to defeat you and disgrace Christ.

The Christian life always involves warfare. Today, there are those who refuse to think or talk about war. In many instances that is understandable. Men's wars are tragic. The soldier can rarely be sure of the real issues. He may not know why he had been called on to do battle, or even whether his cause is just. But there is no such fuzziness about the Christian's warfare. The issues are right up front. In Eden, Satan attacked God's Word. He cast doubt on it (asking history's first question: "Did God say . . . ?"), distorting it ("You can't eat of every tree . . . ?"), and denying it ("You won't die"). To attack God's Word is to attack God. It is to attack Jesus Christ who is the Word made flesh! In response, God declared war on Satan: I will put enmity between (i.e., begin hostilities between) the seed of the woman (Christ and His church) and the seed of the snake (Satan's followers). Thus began— as James R. Graham puts it—the war between the seeds. Warfare between these two opposing camps has raged throughout human history, and it continues today. Like it or not, you are in a war. Every man, woman, and child is lined up on one side or the other. They fight for Christ or they are part of that ungodly brood who fight for the snake. This is a family feud (the bitterest sort of warfare); they are of their father the devil or are part of the family of God. If he doesn't gather (positively work for His cause), he scatters (negatively works against it). He builds up or disorganizes and tears down, whether he realizes it or not.

When a person does recognize his sin, does realize that he is God's enemy, and in repentance lays down his arms and surrenders in faith, he becomes a child of God and joins the Lord's army. He disowns the devil, denounces his cause, and deserts his army. For that reason, the devil especially hates him. He doesn't like his own soldiers, it is true, but deserters who turn and fight against him are the objects of his special dislike. You can be certain therefore that if you have become a Christian, you will raise the ire of the evil one. He'll do all that he can to oppose you and make you ineffective.

Now, you can't do battle with an enemy successfully unless you recognize who he is, that you are truly involved in war, etc. Christians who ignore or forget the fact that they are involved in a cosmic conflict for God cannot fight successfully. The Christian life is a battle; day by day you are engaged in warfare. You must remember this each morning when you crawl from between the sheets. Whether

you do or not will have a lot to do with how the
battle goes that day!

It is easy to forget the war when you are not
always on the front line. Yet some of the most critical war efforts are made behind the lines. You don't
have to be where you hear the rat-a-tat-tat of the
machine guns or the bombs bursting on every side
to be in a war. Christians who are not involved
in the overt activities of the front line also may
tend to forget. Yet, some of the greatest victories
achieved by the other side have taken place because
of carelessness that allowed the enemy to sabotage
the war effort at home.

"What are you talking about? I haven't heard
any bombs bursting and I haven't seen any cloak-
and-dagger stuff either. Why not cut out the melo-
dramatics?" If this is how you see it, Christian,
all I can do is warn you. And I must warn you
sternly, you are endangering not only yourself but
the whole cause of Christ. Wake up! It is when you
don't see such things that you are most vulnerable.
Listen again to Romans 12:21: "Don't be defeated
in battle by evil; but in battle defeat evil with good."
You are in a war, like it or not, and you will be
attacked—one way or another, overtly or subtly.
If you are not ready or ill-prepared you will not be
able to withstand when the attack comes. In some

ways, I'll agree, it is easier where the attack is more overt. When there could be a sniper in every tree you pass, it is easier to stay alert (especially when your buddy just got it yesterday). But this is all the more reason for alertness to the enemies' ways when the dangers seem less imminent. They are no less real, you are no less vital to the effort, and the cause will be no less hurt if you fail.

So, you have been given battle orders by your Commander in Chief: "Don't lose the battle with evil but defeat evil in battle with good." Recognize the fact that you are in a war, and study these orders carefully—there is much in them to help you fight well.

CHAPTER 5

Battle Orders for Today

YOUR BATTLE ORDERS say, "Don't lose; win."
Yet we see so many defeated Christians today. A
Christian woman who had an unsaved husband
regularly attended services at her church. Whenever
anyone asked, "How are you today, Mary?" she'd
answer, "Oh, all right, I suppose. But you know
how hard it is sometimes to live with an unsaved
husband!" At prayer meeting she'd request, "Be sure
to pray for me and John; you know how hard it is
to live with an unsaved husband!" And so it went.
She had built her life around the fact that she was
the "wife of an unsaved husband." It was a life of
defeat, not a life of victory. Consequently when
John got saved, she was furious. The entire structure
of her life had been shattered and she didn't know
what to do. She simply didn't know how to live a
life of victory. All she knew was defeat.

There are many others like this woman. They have built their lives around defeat: "After all, this is a world of sin." But the Bible commands personal victory in the warfare with evil. And that victory is possible. These battle orders are marching orders. They say "move ahead." They command aggressive action. They seek to inculcate a victory mentality. For a Christian to be a defeatist is sin.

Let's examine these battle orders more closely. Every part of them is significant. And unless you thoroughly comprehend and obey them you will lose many battles.

When He established His church, the Lord Jesus said, "The gates of hell will not prevail against it" (Matt. 16:18). Every day, the Christian ought to be rattling the windowpanes of the counsel chambers of the enemy. When God describes Christ's empire in Daniel 7, He says that it would not be taken over by others as previous empires had been. Instead, like a stone, it would grow and grow until it became a huge mountain filling the whole earth. Christ Himself said, "All authority in heaven and earth has been given to me. Go, *therefore*, and make disciples from all nations" (Matt. 28:18, 19). The church is to invade every part of the territory of the evil one taking people captive for Christ as it goes, transforming enemy soldiers into soldiers of the cross, until there are some from "every tribe, and kindred, and language and nation" who know and serve and fight for Jesus Christ. The church was designed for action; it was designed to become a victorious world empire advancing successfully against the enemy. Your task, as one member of the army of His empire, is to defeat the enemy in combat. You are to seize the initiative, take it from the hands of the evil one, and turn him to flight. When Christ came, it was the demons who cried for mercy. The old hymn "Onward, Christian Soldiers" captures the spirit of this verse perfectly: "Marching as to war, with the cross of Jesus going on before." Because of what He did on that cross, where He defeated the devil, you need not fail. I don't care what problem you face; it has no power to defeat the cross of Christ. Christ's soldiers can win—indeed will win—if they follow His marching orders.

You are in a war. Evil must not win. These are your battle orders.

But to be quite clear about it, the second half of the sentence goes further: "You must overcome evil." It is one thing not to lose; it is another to win. You may not come to terms with evil. There can be no truce in which various items are traded off for the sake of peace. You cannot draw a line at the 39th parallel and settle down on your side.

If you do, you can be sure of two things, (1) the enemy will break the truce and (2) your Lord will be disappointed in you. He told you to win the battle, overcome the enemy, not to stop fighting. His battle orders include no directions for drawing up uneasy armistices. He will settle for nothing less than total victory.

Yet Christians are forever trying to arrange cease-fires with Satan. It not only cannot be done; it *should* not be done. Compromise is not in these orders. Everything about them crowds it out. There can be no compromise with sin. This is true whether you are talking about personal sin in your own life, whether you are talking about the sin of trying to compromise with false doctrine, or whether you are talking about compromising God's truth by trying to wed it to some pagan philosophy or system. Everywhere, God calls for victory, not compromise. You must overcome, not overaccommodate!

Are you really overcoming evil in your life? Can you see advance against the enemy? People who seek counseling almost always have allowed evil to overcome them. Many who never go to their pastor for counsel are in the same boat. Are you one of them? Perhaps it is because of your willingness to compromise. In God's world, all cats are not gray. That is because you have been called out of darkness into light. Christ translated you out of darkness into His bright kingdom. One can understand why the non-Christian who has no absolute standard by which to interpret life turns to relativism and settles for compromise whenever he can. At night all cats are gray. But the Christian has the light of Christ shining clearly in His Word; for him life is not yes and no any longer. He has Christ's clear yes; he knows what it is all about and what he must do. He has unmistakable battle orders.

"All of this talk is fine and dandy. But it's not quite so easy as you say. I've tried, but I've also failed. And I haven't heard any real concrete suggestions from you so far either. Are you going to continue to rebuke and exhort throughout, or are you going to give me some plain, helpful direction too? You have no right to get me stirred up like this unless you do." Please be patient. Everything will come in time. I promise I shall not leave you without specific directions. In fact, they may be so specific that you may soon be complaining about that. But all in time. I want first to set the scene.

If your unsaved wife or husband is winning and you are the defeated partner, that is your fault. If you are constantly upset and miserable, don't blame your partner for that. Even though he gives occasion for your failure, it is *your failure* nonetheless.

You *allow* him to win by failing to heed your battle orders. First Peter 3 orders the Christian wife to *win* her husband by her submissive behavior, even if he disobeys the Word. The same is true of the Christian husband. He too must win his unsaved wife by his exercise of Christlike sacrificial loving leadership (cf. v. 7). There is no defeatism in 1 Peter 3.[1] There the Christian is to take the initiative and overcome evil.

You must press the battle to the enemy's doorstep. You are to aggressively attack and defeat him.

---

1. The entire book of 1 Peter has to do with overcoming evil. The message of the book is the same as Rom. 12:21: Evil that causes suffering can be overcome by trusting God and doing what He has commanded (doing good). Study the book in this light, noting how often the themes of suffering and doing right appear. First Peter 3 occurs in a suffering context: Cf. v. 1 "You wives, *likewise*." The word "likewise" refers back to the conclusion of chapter 2 that speaks of how Christ handled persecution.

CHAPTER 6

Is Aggression Christian?

"UNTIL YOU SAID that, I was with you. But now I wonder about your thesis. What do you mean by saying that the Christian must aggressively attack and defeat others? That doesn't sound very Christian to me. I thought the Christian was to turn the other cheek."

When the Bible says "turn the other cheek" it does not forbid aggression. In many ways, turning the other cheek is the most aggressive action that one could take: Paul says it is like heaping coals of fire on another's head. But, again, we'll come to that in time.

The false interpretation of turning the other cheek that equates that action with defeatism, doormatism ("All I can do is lie here and invite you to wipe your muddy boots on me"), pacifism or nonaggression must be exposed for what it is—a non-Christian misrepresentation of the truth. Everywhere, the Bible teaches that the Christian must aggressively fight against evil and overcome it.

The Christian can no more take a passive attitude toward evil than his Lord did. He came into this world to take captivity captive. He came to destroy the works of the evil one and render him powerless (Heb. 2:14). He "disarmed rulers and authorities, made a public display of them, and triumphed over them" (Col. 2:15). There was nothing passive about the cross. He *laid down* His life; it was not *taken* from Him. The cross was active. He was sacrificing Himself for the sins of His people to free them from the chains of sin and the devil. Why then should they willingly submit to these shackles once more?

The Christian is not a Hindu. He doesn't believe in nonviolence or nonaggression. The Christian is the most violent man on earth. He has orders to subdue the enemy and win the victory for His Lord, and he will stop at nothing to do so; his Lord's name is at stake. Look out for a Christian, properly motivated, marching out to battle on orders from Christ! You can't stop him! He's going to win! He's dangerous to the enemy!

The Bible teaches the violent (not nonviolent) overthrow of the enemy. He must be smashed to smithereens, demolished, utterly devastated. No quarter may be given! His power and place are to be destroyed. The Christian position is the most violent and aggressive one of all.

Don't you see? Paul is saying that Christians must invade the enemy's territory and destroy his fortresses (2 Cor. 10:4): "We are destroying speculations and every lofty thing raised up against the knowledge of God." Every defense must be demolished. Nothing can be left standing.

People often ask how the first-century church accomplished so much in so short a time with so few resources. One answer to that question is found in the picture that the church had of itself as a victorious army bent on defeating the enemy for the Lord's sake. Christians in those days saw themselves riding out with the King of kings and His heavenly armies to smite the enemy by the Word of His mouth (Rev. 19:15). That Word powerfully proclaimed by mouth and demonstrated in life is the most aggressive and violent force on earth today. Paul saw himself in this battle. He wrote of himself as "a servant of God" who fought "with weapons of righteousness in the right hand and the left." That is fighting; not passivity!

Light is more aggressive than darkness. Darkness is passive; light is active. Christian, you are one of the people of light—the most aggressive, the most militant force the world has ever known!

CHAPTER 7

The Weapons of Your Warfare

WHEN PAUL WROTE of destroying the enemy's defenses, he also said: "The weapons of our warfare are not of the flesh, but divinely powerful for the destruction of fortresses." In other words, what he was saying fully accords with the assertions that I made in the last chapter. Christians, properly organized and functioning, are the most formidable force in the world because they have the most powerful resources and the finest strategy for using them. They do not depend on fleshly weapons but divinely powerful ones, Paul says.

What does he mean? Much the same thing as when he wrote: "Do not be overcome by evil, but overcome evil *with good*." The Christian is to aggressively—violently—press the battle against the forces of evil until he wins: "overcome evil." But in doing so he may not use just any sort of weapons or any strategy that he wishes. On the contrary, his orders are explicit, God's strategy calls for the use of weapons of righteousness: "overcome evil with good."

The world's methods will not do. The world's weapons are not adequate. The world's strategy must be abandoned. When others do evil you must do good. When others return evil for evil you must return good for evil. These are your Lord's battle orders. You have no choice; you must follow them. He did not leave the planning to you.

Methods—as many Christians wrongly think— are not optional, or unimportant. In some ways they are most important of all. Good plans can be ruined by bad methods of carrying them out. Good ideas can be distorted by conflicting ways of actualizing them. Methods, ways and means, etc., must be in harmony with intentions. That is why Christ specified: "overcome evil *with good.*"

Christ will countenance no other way of defeating evil. Evil must be overcome His way. Any other way would be too feeble and would be out of harmony with His holy intentions. Evil must be met and conquered on the field of battle with good. Good is the most powerful, most aggressive, most violent force one could possibly use.

Why can't the Christian return abuse in kind? I have already indicated that if he did he would be using a strategy and ways and means that are contrary to Christ's purposes. That would be a poor way to wage war indeed. If the Christian attempted to overcome evil with evil rather than with good, if he retaliated in kind, he would be spreading evil even more widely and thus defeating His major objective—to defeat evil. You simply cannot overcome evil by spreading about more of the same!

Nevertheless, there are Christians everywhere who in practice (if not in principle) seem to think otherwise. "I'll get even," "Well, why shouldn't I? Look what he did to me," "I was only doing what he did to me" are sentiments that every counselor regularly hears fall from the lips of Christians. But they shouldn't. Perhaps you have been acting out of a similar spirit. If so, it is time for you to recognize the fact and begin to think seriously about Christ's orders: "Overcome evil with good." Quite seriously, have you ever made a concerted effort to do so? Do you even know how to do so? If you can't answer yes to these questions you are not unlike many other Christians. No wonder the church lacks power, finds itself faced with much legitimate criticism, and so often fails to push back the forces of evil!

This passage of Scripture was given by the Holy Spirit for the express purpose of telling you *what* to do and *how* to do it. Before we have finished our exploration of Romans 12:14–21 you will know both. By God's grace I trust you also will *do* what you learn. What you read will be of little benefit otherwise. It is tragic to be convicted of failure to do what you know God wants you to do and to go no farther.

There is another reason why the Christian must not return abuse in kind. Not only does this put him at cross-purposes with the intentions of His Lord because it is out of harmony with His divine strategy, but it also puts him out of touch with His divine power. It is not simply that Christ refuses to bless and empower the Christian when he disobeys His battle orders—that is true enough—but it is also true that evil does not have the power that good does.

When the Christian goes to war, he must use God's weapons God's way. God, in His wisdom, has commanded the use of good. It is by doing good—spreading light rather than darkness—that you are called to rout the enemy. Only good has power enough to effectuate this.

The enemy is deeply entrenched. He is powerful and well armed. He is highly skilled in the use of his own weapons. He knows his strategy well. Evil is a formidable force. Its power must not be underestimated. Its potential to fight and fight well must not be minimized. Because Christ does not train His troops in the use of evil, they are sitting ducks for the enemy when they try to use the enemy's methods. They are ill-suited to such fighting tactics. The forces of evil can do (and have done) much harm in this world. The history of mankind is—from one perspective—largely the history of destruction brought about by evil. That is why the Christian who tries to combat the enemy on his own terms is a fool.

But he doesn't have to do so. Christ has provided ways and means that He blesses when they are used in His name according to the directions of His Word. Evil is powerful, but good is more powerful. In fact, evil is so powerful that only good has the power to overcome evil. Darkness can be driven away only by light. That is why the Christian will fail to achieve His purposes if he uses any lesser force.

Good is so much more powerful than evil that, by comparison, evil is but a popgun. Good, in contrast, is a nuclear weapon. What a tragedy, then, to see Christian soldiers, for whom God has provided such an arsenal, running about the battlefield with popguns with little corks dangling from a string at the end of the barrel! If it were not so tragic, it would be ludicrous to picture Christians in possession of weapons that are "divinely powerful" cringing on their knees in front of the enemy's popguns.

Yet that is the picture. When Christians fear evil and evildoers, they do so only because they are unsure or unskilled in the use of their own weapons. There is no other reason for doing so. While the power of evil is real, it is no longer to be considered power at all by comparison with the power of God. Don't be afraid of that unsaved mother-in-law, that unsaved boss, that unsaved husband, that unsaved teenager or parents. What can they do to you if you oppose their evil deeds with good? Before good pursued consistently, faithfully, and vigorously, the enemy at length will turn in defeat. Christ says "overcome evil with good" because that is the way it can be done! You are destined to be a winner; Christian, begin to demonstrate your destiny now.

Do you believe this, Christian? Does it all seem too easy, too unrealistic, too simplistic? Well, let me ask you this, how well are you making out in your battles with evil now, using the world's methods and weapons? Can't say you're doing too well, can you? Then trust God and forget your fears and doubts. Take God's weapons in hand and throw yourself wholeheartedly into the fray. Depend on the great General's strategy. Stop trying to think things out for yourself. Look where that has got you. You are a soldier in the army, not its leader. You have received orders from headquarters. Heed them. They are not yours to question; they have been given to follow. Don't run the risk of being found guilty of insubordination—to Christ!

And, as we leave this consideration for a time, reflect on one thing: the cross is the supreme example of returning good for evil. In it, the greater power of good can be seen most clearly. Here in its supreme manifestation, evil gathered together all its resources and flung them into the face of God's Son. Yet, what was the outcome? You know the answer, good gloriously triumphed over evil. Not only did Christ transform the cross into a stepping stone to the resurrection, but the very death by which good seemed defeated instead brought about the ultimate destruction of sin and Satan. What Christian, thinking clearly about the meeting of good and evil at the cross, can ever seriously doubt the greater power of good? Yes, you know that Paul's words are true—profoundly true—because you have experienced its effects in salvation.

CHAPTER 8

Your Mouth Is
a Problem

SO FAR WE HAVE BEEN considering the last
verse of Romans 12:14–21. This verse is a sum-
mary that in a more general way encapsulates what
has come before. Because of its general and more
abstract nature, I have looked at it first to set the
theme, establish the mood, and color the whole.
Paul is thinking of the battle with evil in military
terms. He lets us know that we are in a war, we
are not to lose any battles, and we need not do so
as long as we obey our battle orders and use God's
weapons and strategy. Indeed, we may not settle for
a cease-fire, but we are to vigorously and violently
demolish all the fortifications of the foe, winning
the battle and taking him captive for Christ. The
church is not to assume a defensive posture, but

51

take aggressive action to *overcome* evil by means
of good.

This general discussion was necessary because
we had to be sure of general principles first. Now,
as we go back and work through verses 14–20 we
shall discover the particulars that lead to the con-
clusions to which verse 21 alludes. Remember, in
all that follows, there is one guiding principle that
looms largest in the passage: the Christian vigorously overcomes evil *by doing good.* This one principle permeates verses 14–20.

If you have been impatiently waiting for specific directions, then you are about to be satisfied.
In verse 14, Paul becomes quite concrete. He says,
"Bless those who persecute you; bless and curse
not." Paul, like James,[1] is keenly aware of the
primary place of communication. In Ephesians
4:25–31, before dealing with specific issues in
human relationships, Paul first considers the need
for and principles of Christian communication.
His general theme for chapters 4–6 is the Christian walk. But he knows that for people to walk
together they first must learn to talk together.
Similarly, here the communication response to
evil comes first. It is useless to try anything else
until this area has been explored. All the good

1. James 3:1-12.

intentions in the world, all the efforts that might be made, all this can be undone by one careless word. Reflective communication, that unique gift with which God endowed man, and by which He enabled him to relate to Himself and to his neighbor as no animal could, tragically, as the result of sin, has become the means by which men have incurred the deepest hurts and alienation of all. So then, the Christian *must* learn how to communicate with those who wrong him.

Paul's additional words, "Bless and curse not," make it clear that you and I aren't by nature the kinds of persons who find it easy to obey this battle order. His words indicate that we would find it much easier to curse than to bless a persecutor. I think that we shall have to admit that he is absolutely right in this assessment of us. What he is calling for, then, is radical change. It is a change that once effected, you can see would make you quite different. It would transform your personality. Indeed, you may wonder whether such change is possible, since it would mean so great an adjustment in your way of doing things. Remember: every command of God brings hope since God never asks His children to do anything that they can't do if they follow biblical directions and draw on the power and resources of His Spirit. Yes, you *can* learn to bless those who persecute you if you are a child of God.

Of course, you were born the kind of person who wants to return evil for evil, cursing for cursing (whether you actually do so to one's face or not). You may not regularly follow through on your inner desires out of fear of consequences, expediency, etc., but in your mind or under your breath more than once you may have said (to borrow Bob Newhart's phrase): "Same to you, fella!" You, as a sinner, were born with a snarling attitude. Somebody snaps at you; you snap back. Somebody pulls your hair; you pull his. Somebody lies to you; you lie to him. It is that attitude that Paul says must change: "You must walk no longer as the gentiles walk" (Eph. 4:17). Actually, Paul is merely echoing Jesus' no to sinful retaliation (cf. Luke 6:27, 28; Matt. 5:44).

Instead, the Christian's response must be to return good (blessing) for evil (cursing). Clearly, blessing is a positive, aggressive response, not a passive one. It is akin to turning the other cheek. One doesn't turn the cheek in every sense, only in the sense of returning good for evil. He has sinned. You give the other person the opportunity to repent and do the right thing instead. You do not turn him off. In effect, by returning good for evil, you are demanding better of him than he has given you thus far. You aggressively refuse to accept his sinful behavior and thrust forth your other cheek for a kiss rather than a slap. Here, rather than curse the curser, you bless the curser; instead of turning him off, you hang in there, and with a soft answer, attempt to turn away wrath. You show care for him by your blessing. You show concern for his attitude and sinful speech and give him the opportunity to respond to your blessing in a similar manner.

That is not passivity. That is an active, aggressive, demanding response that requires something different from the persecutor. Doing good to another involves the most violent sort of attack on him. It is a pointed thrust at his basic stance toward you and ultimately toward God (in whose name you bless).

When you do good you show love toward another. Love is structured by God's commandments. Love is not a formless, jelly-like thing; it takes a distinct shape in each context, a shape that is molded by the Word of God. Doing good (i.e., doing whatever God's Word defines as good and requires of us), then, is showing love. But again, love—like light—is a powerful, positive force. Love attacks hatred like light attacks darkness.

And love is a force that never fails. Nothing can dislodge it or cause it to cease. Unendingly, it endures all things, believes all things, hopes all things. Such a spirit built into the blessing of others is unconquerable. And it is irresistible, too.

Love is not first a feeling. Though the feelings come later and grow thick in the basic loam of love, they don't constitute the sum and substance of love. Love is doing whatever good God says you must do for another, to please God, whether (at first) it pleases you or not. You must do so because He says so; and you don't wait until you feel like doing so. Love begins with obedience toward God in which one gives to another whatever the other needs. Love is not a gooey, sticky sentimental thing; it is hard to love. Often it hurts to love. Love meant going to the cross through the garden of Gethsemane. Christ did not feel like dying for your sins, Christian, but He did so nonetheless. The Scriptures teach that He *endured* the cross while focusing on the subsequent joy that it would bring. Often as you express love, you fix your eyes too much on goals and objectives beyond the immediate circumstances. More must be said about this matter later on.

We are concerned in verse 14 with how love talks. How does God want the Christian to respond verbally to a persecutor? The passage says, "Bless those who persecute you." The persecution in view might encompass persecution of various sorts. Since other types of persecution will be considered later, I shall *focus* here on verbal persecution. I make this emphasis because in this verse we also are talking about verbal responses to persecution. Moreover, the sort of persecution that Christians most frequently encounter in America is verbal and social, not physical. It is not easy to control your tongue under such conditions, and that is where much damage is done. Love will teach you how to manage your mouth.

Now notice, Paul doesn't say "*if* you are persecuted." No. He assumes that you will be. The matter is beyond debate. The Scriptures teach that "all those who want to live godly in Christ Jesus will be persecuted" (2 Tim. 3:12). As Jesus put it, "In the world you will have tribulation" (John 16:33). But He goes on in the same verse to say, "But take heart; I have overcome the world." The implication is that as He has overcome the world so too can His followers. He overcame evil with good; we too must do so.

Persecution, according to the witness of both Christ and Paul, comes to Christians (Paul seems to indicate that the more godly one becomes, the more likely it is that persecution will increase). Every

Christian (if truly a Christian), no matter how hard he tries to hide his Christianity, will slip sometime! Then persecution will come. Slander, abuse, mockery, insults; all these and more are part and parcel of verbal persecution. And those who don't mind putting their Christianity in the display case where all can see it will all the more suffer persecution. The more a Christian lives like Christ, the more he will suffer like Christ. I am not talking about the sort of snobbish lifestyle that provokes attacks. Rather, Christians are to be "as wise as snakes and as harmless as doves" (suave and careful, but not deceitful or deceptive). If you haven't suffered sometime, somehow for your faith, then either (1) you are not a Christian at all, (2) you are not living as a Christian should, or (3) suffering may be around the next bend in your road. So, if persecution is certain, the Christian must know how to handle it and be prepared to do so. Christ suffered persecution for trying to live in a godly manner, but He overcame the world by doing good.

Who is persecuting you? Who is cursing you (by slander, gossip, words of personal abuse, etc.)? Is it your next-door neighbor? Did a friend say those nasty words that stung? Was it a family member who told you off? What about the gossip that is being spread by an in-law? Did your mother-in-law tell you to mind your own business? Some of the most bitter words of all are spoken by ambivalent family members who also love you most deeply. How about your husband or wife? Your parents or children? Have you had words with a boss or business associate? Who is it? Think now, and ask yourself, "How can I handle it? Did I bless those who cursed? Did I curse? What did I do?"

Do any of the following responses come close to what you said (or thought—remember, in thoughts we speak to ourselves): "In straight unvarnished words, let me tell you what you can do about your complaint. As far as I'm concerned, you can . . . ," "Is that so? Well, let me tell you a thing or two," "John, do you know what Bill said about you?" "Yeah? Well, let me tell you all about him!" "Really, Mary, don't you think that purple tablecloths are a bit too busy for the fellowship supper?" "Not nearly as busy as people who poke their noses into the affairs of committees to which they don't belong!" or finally, "I really blessed him!" (Note how as sinners we even take the language of this biblical verse and disgracefully distort it!)

As a sinner who has developed sinful response patterns (a sinner could do nothing else), you have developed a sinful style of responding to those who address you in ways you don't like.

The sinful cursing response is inborn. My son, before he had an adequate vocabulary, invented his own curses. As a youngster he loved trucks. One day, incensed at what a friend had done, he said, "You . . . you dump truck with a wheel off!" He is not alone. Because of social pressure, more often that not, you may find the curse (not always phrased in cursing vocabulary) come up and stick just behind your front teeth. That has been your tendency for some time. It will be hard to change. Even if you are now a Christian, you may continue to struggle with those former speech response patterns.

A friend who had refereed hundreds of games between Bible colleges tells me that in the crunch, again and again he has heard the curse come out. It is not easy to overcome habits. But it is possible. Let's consider how.

CHAPTER 9

How to Manage
Your Mouth

FIRST, WE MUST understand the serious nature of a curse. Then, motivated by this realization, we shall see what can be done about it. I hope we too shall see something of the great benefits of blessing.

Do you know what a curse is? What a blessing is? When you curse, you virtually invoke God's judgment on another. When you say "damn you" (or its equivalent), you are asking God to send the person you have cursed to hell forever. You are so angry that you would like him to suffer the torments and punishments of eternal wrath. That's your *spirit*; that's your *attitude* at the moment—no matter how you phrase your thoughts (words to yourself) and speech (words to others). When you say under your breath (or to his face), "I'd like to wring your neck," the spirit of murderous cursing is there.

A curse ought not issue from your heart or mouth lightly; God may listen. Is that what you *really* want God to do—damn him forever in hell? Cursing is serious business. When you take time to think about hell, and what it is like to suffer its torments forever, can you stick to the thoughts and words of the moment? Such words ought never to slip from a believer's lips; in time they should even disappear from his heart and mind.

James points out how tragic, contradictory, and incongruent it is for a believer to curse another. "Out of the same mouth come words that bless God and words that curse men." Then he says, "This ought not to be!" He makes the point vividly: "The same stream doesn't send forth brackish water and sweet water!" (James 3:9–10). A believer is the only one who understands what hell is and what freedom from the fear of bondage in hell is all about (Heb. 2:14, 15). Surely, then, he should be the last to curse his neighbor. He knows that he would be under God's eternal curse if Christ had not died to free him from it by bearing his hell for him on the cross. He knows that it is a "terrifying thing to fall into the hands of the living God." How then can a Christian curse?

The curse may be spoken before God alone, as when one speaks only to himself (but in God's presence, of course), or it also may be spoken before men. The curse may be the invoking of God's wrath privately or publicly. Either way it is a curse, but it surely includes the private curse as well. The private curse doesn't include the public, but the public curse always includes the thoughts and the intents of the heart. Both are condemned in this passage.

"I can see that such attitudes and words are utterly inconsistent with my Christian faith, but how do I stop cursing; what will change me?" The Lord Jesus Christ has told us that we must put off our own desires and follow Him. In that twofold call to discipleship you have the essence of all life change. You can't stop cursing. That is impossible. Rather, you must *replace* cursing with something else. Sinful ways do not just disappear. Their habitual nature is too difficult to dislodge when replaced only by a vacuum. Instead they must be shoved out by new righteous ways that please God. The Christian—because in Christ he has already put off sin and put on righteousness (Col. 3)—alone can replace sinful ways with holy ones. Because of the Holy Spirit's presence it is possible for him to change at a level of depth. He may truly learn how to please God by becoming and acting like (and acting like and becoming) the kind of person who does please Him. It is possible for the regenerate person to replace old sinful ways with biblical alternatives.

The alternative to cursing is clearly spelled out: "*Bless* those who persecute you. *Bless* and don't curse." You will change when instead of cursing you have learned to bless. It is one thing to try to stop cursing; it is quite another to start blessing. Cursing (inward and outward) will cease when blessing (inward and outward) truly replaces it.

The change will not come overnight. One must discipline himself for godliness. That means constant awareness of God's demand for blessing, consistent desire to please Him, and continued effort to bless rather than curse. It is in the regular doing that the renewal will take place. The old ways will be shed as the new ones become dominant. The new leaven must be worked into the dough of your life. Regular, conscious, obedient effort must come first. Then, at length, the unconscious blessing response will follow.

Well, then, what is a blessing? It is not enough merely to say that it is the opposite of a curse, though that is true enough. Let's be quite specific. To bless another is to ask God to do good to him; indeed, it is to ask God to save him and work other good changes in his life. It is to ask God to show mercy on him in spite of what he has done to you. To bless is to pray for those who spitefully use you. It is to ask God to do good to those who do evil to you. And this may be done publicly or privately too.

Christ on the cross prayed for those who killed Him; later, Stephen did the same (clearly, then, this is not something that only perfect persons can do). These blessings[1] were in essence prayers for the greatest good of the persecutor: "Father, forgive them" (Luke 23:34), "Don't hold this sin against them" (Acts 7:60). Were these blessing-prayers, invoking God's salvation on others, answered? On Pentecost (and on subsequent occasions mentioned in Acts) those for whom Christ prayed were "pierced in their hearts" as Peter preached, "You, with wicked hands have slain the Lord of Glory!" They cried out, "What must we do?" Then Peter led them to Christ and great numbers were saved. As God's answer to Stephen's prayer, the greatest missionary and preacher of all time—Paul—was converted.

In 1 Peter 2:21–23 the Christian is called on to handle persecution as Christ did: When He was

---

1. Note that "pray" is used synonymously with "bless" in Matt. 5:44.

reviled (cursed), He didn't revile in return and He uttered no threats (curses).

"Well," you say, "If I bless another rather than give him back the same as he gave me I'll look like a fool." That is altogether possible, perhaps even probable. But so what? Paul said that he looked like a fool—for Christ's sake (cf. 1 Cor. 4:10). This verse is frequently quoted by Christians, but rarely quoted in context. Among those things that Paul said made him such a fool was that "when we are reviled, we bless; when we are persecuted, we endure; when we are slandered, we try to conciliate" (1 Cor. 4:12, 13). It is, of course, better to look like a fool or to be called a fool than to be one. The person who disobeys the clear will of God in this matter is, in the long run, the one who not only looks like a fool, but turns out to be one.

According to Proverbs 26:4, when you return curse for curse you are a fool, because the fool is one who answers a fool according to his folly (i.e., in kind). The Christian who returns blessing for cursing answers a fool in a way that exposes him for such and puts down his pride rather than becoming like him (26:5).

Do you mind being thought of as a fool when you realize that they thought the same of Paul? Even more so, what do you care if men call you a fool for acting like your heavenly Father? In Matthew 5:44, 45, Christ commands, "Love your enemies and pray for those who persecute you."[2] Then he continues "in order that you may be sons of your Father in heaven[3] since He causes His sun to rise on the evil and the good and sends rain on the righteous and the unrighteous" (i.e., he returns good for evil). The Christian is to be perfect as He is (i.e., by returning good for evil). In the book of Romans, Paul describes this goodness of God toward wicked men and attributes to it a motive to lead them to repentance (Rom. 2:4).

Love—and that's what we've been talking about—always says something different from what another has said to you. Outwardly (or under your breath), you speak to God and to other men words that seek their welfare. Love always focuses on the welfare of the other person rather than one's self. It never "seeks its own" (1 Cor. 13:5). This shift in focus from self to the other person is critical. It is one of the principal factors that make the Christian response possible. When our concerns are focused only on our own hurts, it is easy to fall into self-pity

2. See previous footnote.
3. One does not become a son of God by good works; he manifests that sonship as real thereby.

and to spiral downward into depression.[4] Without this focus it is all but impossible to return good for evil. But when one begins to think about the sin of the persecutor and begins to concern himself for the other's welfare enough to bless and pray for him, he is well on his way toward developing a compassion for him too.

So then, in all of this, the emphasis is on the *other* person, not on yourself (your hurt, your pain, etc.). That is the way of love. And that is the way to bless rather than curse. Your concerns must be, "What can I do *for* (not *to*) him? How can I respond in a way that does him the most good? If he is persecuting you, clearly he needs help. Think, "Here is a person far from God; what can I do and say to him to bring him to God?" You can't do anything for yourself anyway, so why focus on your welfare? Leave *that* to God; He is concerned about you and will care for you (cf. 1 Peter 4:19—entrust yourself to God, and do what is right). As God's focus is on you, your focus must be on the welfare of the persecutor.

You have wanted to know how it is possible to return good works for evil. I have pointed out

---

4. See my *Competent to Counsel, The Christian Counselor's Manual, What about Nouthetic Counseling?* etc. for further information on the depression spiral.

some of the facts involved. Other principles will emerge as we discus the verses that follow. But basically let me say that the renewal of your life that the Holy Spirit is effecting comes as you read and obey the Scriptures. As you read expectantly, the Spirit will use His Word to change and remake your life. You must become aware of His requirements. That awareness comes through hearing that Word in faith, and that awareness leads to conviction of sin. This conviction leads to correction (through confession and repentance), and correction must be followed by disciplined training in righteousness (i.e., in the response patterns required by God). This four-step process of change is brought about by the Spirit using His Word (cf. 2 Tim. 3:15–17).[5]

Earlier I asked you to think about who has been persecuting you. Did you? Then you may need to do several things if you have not already done so:

1. If you cursed him in return, seek forgiveness from God and from him.
2. If your focus has been on yourself rather than on your persecutor, ask for God's

---

5. For a more detailed explanation of this passage and the process that it describes see my book, *The Christian Counselor's Manual*, 3, 93, 212, 23, 158, 187, 233.

forgiveness and begin to think about his needs. (These are clearly indicated in his words and actions toward you, if you have the eyes to see them.)

3. Ask God to save and help him. Pray specifically for his welfare.

4. Think of kindly, good, helpful words that you can speak to him now (and on later occasions).

You will learn to manage your mouth in stress situations only by focusing on the other person and blessing rather than cursing. The curse always reveals self-focus, self-centeredness. That is your basic concern. When you successfully fight this battle in your own heart, you will find the battle outside going well. Both go hand in hand. You cannot fight the inner battle with self-centeredness, pride, and your mouth unless you begin to bless others. And, blessing others helps to turn the focus from yourself. You cannot be cursing when you are truly blessing.

Learn God's way to manage your mouth!

CHAPTER 10

You Can't Fight Alone

IT IS PROBABLY time to recapitulate a bit. I began by looking rather extensively at Romans 12:21, which sums up what Paul has been saying in verses 14 through 20. He writes: "Don't be overcome by evil, but overcome evil with good."

That means you are in a war with evil, and that you must not be defeated in your battles with the forces of evil that oppose you. Indeed, you are to win all those battles and seek to take the enemy captive for Christ. But this can be done only if you use God's great battle plan: "overcome evil with good." The world doesn't believe in this kind of warfare, doesn't know anything about it, and is unprepared to handle it. It will take your opponent unawares; it is God's secret weapon. Unsaved persons may scoff at the idea of turning the other cheek[1] and doing good in response to evil, but when they are faced with an actual case where a Christian does so, they are nonplussed by it. This is God's plan for overcoming and destroying evil. You must destroy evil with good. How else could it be overcome, when you think about it? There are just two options—you can respond to evil with more evil or you can respond with good. You must go one way or the other, and everyone does. If you try to destroy evil with evil you spread more of the same, thereby enlarging rather than destroying it. You may not do evil that good may come (Rom. 3:8). Good doesn't come from evil. Evil produces only evil; only good produces good. This, we saw, begins with our verbal response (vocal or subvocal), in which we do good by blessing/praying rather than returning curse for curse. The Christian talks to God first, focusing on the persecutor's welfare, then says good things to the persecutor himself.

Now we turn to verse 15: "Rejoice with those who rejoice, and weep with those who weep." In

---

1. Not, of course, to be hit again (God doesn't want you to encourage anyone to go on sinning!), but in order to give the offender a second opportunity (this time to do the *right* thing). A good response to evil puts tremendous pressure on the offender to reexamine his attitudes. God often uses it to bring conviction of sin.

overcoming evil with good, you quickly discover that there is also evil within the church that needs to be overcome. In order to root it out, so that Christ's army will be strong and effective, each member must learn to identify with others. We need each other, and to meet those needs we must come close to one another. The church must be an army in which the soldiers are sensitive to each other. You simply can't fight the battles alone. Neither can others in Christ's church. You need each other's resources. That is why Paul writes: "Rejoice with those who rejoice, and weep with those who weep."

In this battle against the forces of evil we need each other. An army doesn't consist of one person alone. You must fight side by side with fellow soldiers of Jesus Christ. You must stand *with* them, not just fight as so many separate individuals. Rather, in your love and concern, you must flow together with them as drops of a liquid in the same glass.

To rejoice and weep with others means that you must develop an empathy that grows from allowing their concerns to overlap and, when necessary, to supersede your own. It is the attitude of Christ, expressed so vividly in Philippians 2:3–11, that must prevail. He allowed concern for us—miserable sinners that we were (and so it doesn't matter what your brother or sister is like)—to override His own. This same attitude is to be in you that was in Him (Phil. 2:5). Then you will help others to stand with you, strengthening them in the battle and enjoying in return the strength that they impart to you.

You cannot go it alone. There is no such thing as a lone wolf Christian. The monk in the monastery or the ascetic in the cave who tries to shut off others so that he may devote himself to God alone fails. He fails because he was made to be a social creature: "It is not good for man to be alone" (Gen. 2:18). And he fails because he cannot obey the second great commandment: "love your neighbor as yourself." The apostle John astutely observes that "the one who does not love his brother whom he has seen, cannot love God whom he has not seen" (1 John 4:20). So you *must* become involved with others who are fighting at your side.

This verse makes it clear that the church is really one. When you love another person, you enter into his life. His concerns become your concerns too. If Joe goes to the hospital to have a tumor removed from his brain, others in the congregation feel something of the agony and heartache that Joe and his family feel. They enter into the fear and concern and care about the financial burdens that this illness has brought with it. Because they have shared in this family's concerns, they "weep with those who weep." That means not only to share in the emotional experience of the family's loneliness as Joe leaves for the hospital, but it also means to think about their needs and become involved in their problems enough to *do* something about them. It may mean to give money, time, effort, etc. To "weep with those who weep" is a powerful concept.

And yet, often that is the easiest thing to do. You can get a group of people to come together for a special prayer meeting almost any time when somebody is rushed to the hospital. But could you get the same group to come together to thank God for Joe's recovery and "rejoice with those who rejoice"? More to the point, suppose that instead of coming home from the hospital Joe had just gotten a raise in salary—a raise that the family greatly needed. This raise would give him new resources from which to give to the church, enable him to serve and witness better, and meet the needs of the family. Envy and jealousy might even get in the way of rejoicing him. But why shouldn't it be as easy to get together to rejoice with those who rejoice? Identification with others in *both* positive and negative situations is commanded, and we must learn to experience both. When you find it as spontaneously easy to rejoice with others who rejoice as freely as you weep with those who weep, you will know that you have learned to do what God requires of you.

Perhaps Luke 15 is the clearest example of this problem. There Jesus makes it plain that there is a widespread failure to rejoice with others who rejoice. Sour grapes is more likely to result. The pouting elder brother is typical of it. There are three parables in this chapter, and all three hang together. In each, the parables of the sheep, the coin, and the brother, something is lost and found. The point of each is not the salvation of the sheep, the coin, or the brother, although that enters into the parable. The main point lies elsewhere.

First, a sheep is lost and the shepherd goes look-ing for it. He finds it, gathers all the other shepherds together, and they rejoice. That's right; that's what they ought to do.

Then, the woman loses her coin. She searches all over for it and finally finds it. Then she gathers all of her women friends together and they have a shindig over it. They rejoice. That's right; that's what they ought to do.

Finally, the father seeks his lost son and finds him. He throws a party and kills the fattened calf. That's right; that's what they ought to do. Then—all of a sudden—a negative note is sounded. The older brother appears, inquires about these happenings, and on hearing what has taken place goes off in a huff. He refuses even to enter the house. He pouts rather than rejoices. The Pharisees were like that. Jesus went seeking the lost, but they complained that He was eating with tax collectors and sinners; they would not rejoice with the angels. That is how a lot of Christians respond to the good news of others. But that's wrong; that's what they ought *not* to do!

This spirit cannot continue if the Lord's army wants to win His battles. There must be a unity that grows out of sympathetic concern of one soldier for another. We must first learn to do good to one another if we want to be able to do good to unbelievers who persecute us. You will never learn to battle the enemy with goodness if you haven't learned how to do good to your friends. Doing good comes from entering into the joys and sorrows of others. It means, as we have seen, learning to focus on the other person's needs rather than on our own.[2] The easiest place to begin doing this is among friends.

2. Cf, chapter 18 for more on this point.

The capacity to weep and to rejoice with others doesn't come by osmosis. It is impossible to enter into their lives unless you take the time and make the effort to get to know them. One of the greatest problems Christians have today is a lack of fellowship with one another. If you don't know Joe, you can't know his sorrows or his joys. Again, we are so wrapped up in our own concerns that we have no time to become concerned about others. If you want to weep and rejoice as you should, you will find it necessary to take the time to cultivate and develop close ties with those around you. That means doing things together, spending time in each other's homes, etc. No wonder the army is weak when Christians can see each other once a week in structured services only and never get to know each other.

How well tuned are you to the needs of other Christians? What are you doing to remedy the situation? Today, why not make some plan for fellowship with another brother or sister? If you don't come up with a better suggestion, why not get on the phone and call up Phil or Patty and invite them over for dessert following next Sunday's evening service?

CHAPTER 11

You Are Part of God's Army

YOU NEED OTHERS in overcoming evil, and they need you. You need them all; all of them need you. Again and again counselors see defeated Christians who fail to call on others who could have helped. Instead, they get themselves into all sorts of unnecessary tangles from which it is hard to disentangle them.

In our study of verse 15, "Rejoice with those who rejoice and weep with those who weep," we saw that in order to press the battle against the foe, we who know Christ need to stand together. The unity that is needed grows out of a cultivation of mutual sensitivity and concern. To use Paul's frequently occurring image, the church must become a well-functioning body in which the concerns of

79

one part influence the other parts. If a thumb is injured, the whole body is affected by it.

The kind of empathy described in verse 15 means to "feel together," but it does not mean to face the same situation, or to do so in the same way that another does. True empathy means to enter fully into the impact of another's situation, but to help him in it always means you must take a different approach than he if he is failing to meet it as he should. You will be of no help if you say, "I suppose that you are doing all you can." Indeed, if he is defeated by his circumstances, you *know* that he is not doing all that God requires. So you may have to confront him with the alternatives that the Bible offers. In fact, the more deeply that you feel his problem, or the more deeply you enter into his joy, the more you will realize what sorts of things he needs to learn from the Scriptures. Just as you must enter into sympathetic disagreement with a brother who says "there's no hope,"[1] so you too must empathetically disagree with the one who fails to thank God for what he rejoices about, acting as if he obtained his blessing on his own. So then, in either direction, it must be remembered, empathy is the rule. But empathy

1. Cf. my *What about Nouthetic Counseling?* for a fuller explanation of empathetic disagreement.

does not mean simple agreement. Empathy, at its deepest level, means entering into the situation profoundly enough to discover the areas that one's brother or sister has failed to see, and caring enough to disagree with his or her hopelessness or persistence in an unbiblical course of action. That, in a nutshell, is what rejoicing and weeping in verse 15 may boil down to.

Now we come to verse 16: "Be of the same mind toward one another. Do not be haughty in mind, but associate with lowly things. Do not be wise in your own estimation." There are three things here. All three are of significance to getting along with others in the King's army. Let's take up each separately.

"Be of the same mind toward one another." This doesn't mean that every Christian must think exactly alike. The word *mind* in the Scriptures doesn't refer to the intellectual processes alone (as so often it does in modern speech and thought). Rather, it refers to the inner man, the life carried on beneath the skin. Often, it seems to be akin to our word "attitude"; and that is probably the sense in which Paul uses the word here. You must have the same attitude toward God, the world, and one another. Basically, your goals and aspirations should be similar. You and other Christians depend on the same source of information (the Bible), have available the same power (the Holy Spirit), and have the same fundamental objective (to glorify God). You all have the same foe. So, there should be a unanimity of attitude.

The one thing that the Lord's army must not have is dissension in the ranks. There is a common enemy; it is he—not one another—that you must fight! That is the point Paul wishes to make: be in harmony—that is what being "of the same mind toward one another" means. "Divide and conquer" is an old tactic of the evil one. Paul wants you to guard against it; don't be taken in by the devil's strategy. God wants to see His troops standing shoulder to shoulder in the face of the foe.

The squabbles that so often are seen in the church are most debilitating to her work. Much time and energy that could be utilized in the Lord's work, is wasted instead on infighting. Wounded by one another, weak and discouraged by battles among themselves, the soldiers of Christ grimly limp forth against the enemy. No wonder their spirits are crushed, no wonder they are glad if they can but hold their own, no wonder the ring of victory is so seldom heard. It is not the enemy who is defeating us; it is we ourselves. How important it is, then, if you want to be sharp and alert and fresh enough to overcome evil with good, to heed this command. There must be good morale among the members of Christ's army, and you must contribute to it!

"How may I go about it?" you ask. Consider a parallel passage: Philippians 2. There was division in the Philippian church (Philippians 4:1ff.). Paul calls the church to unity (1:27–2:12). In the heart of this he says, "Let this mind [attitude] be in you that was in Christ Jesus." What sort of attitude did He have?

It is an attitude he describes this way: Christians must (like Christ) look on others as more important than themselves and must show more concern for their interests than for their own. That is what Christ did. Rather than hold on to the heavenly privileges that were His, He laid them all aside, became a man (a slave), and was crucified *for the sake of others.* He put your interests before His own. For this God highly exalted Him, calling Him "Lord."

If someone has gifts for music or leadership that are greater than your own, you must recognize these, push the other person forward, possibly urging him/her to replace you; rather than become jealous over his/her threat of vying for ascendency.

Putting others first also means praying that Joe will get that raise. It means praying that God will bless other believers in concrete ways, and rejoicing when He does. So, you can see how important is the command to "be of the same mind" (i.e., to live harmoniously). It is obeyed when others develop the practice of putting other Christians and their interests first. Often it will mean stepping down to assist others as a servant (like our Lord: "the Son of man came to serve") instead of seeking the position of prominence.

This leads into the second command: "Do not be haughty in mind, but associate with the lowly" (or possibly "with lowly things"). Who is number one in your life? Is it you or Christ? Who is number two? Is it you or others? The haughty person thrusts himself into the limelight, takes the place of prominence, doesn't know how to step down, and has little or nothing to do with less prominent persons. He is, in his own estimation, number one (or soon will be).

Rather, says Paul, you can't have all captains in the Lord's army. Many persons are needed for the day-by-day normal activities that are required to sustain an army and to make war. For everyone to aspire to be in places of leadership, to seek wealth, power, or fame would be disastrous. Instead, each must be willing to take a humble place—peeling spuds, if need be—happily serving Christ in whatever ways he can. It is the Lord Himself Who must move you up higher. Be willing to do simple, mundane things for Christ.

While I am delighted over the so-called "lay" movements of your day, in which everyday man-in-the-pew believers are entering into the work of Christ with new vigor, I am concerned to some extent over laymen taking on tasks too readily and moving ahead into places of prominence too rapidly. It is important for the church to ordain to authority those who have the gifts for leadership (there must be more alertness to emerging leadership and, when proven, a greater willingness to acknowledge it by ordination). But it is also of importance for unordained persons not to set themselves up to do the world *of* the elder or the deacon *over against* the rightful leaders in the congregation. You can't have a private first class assuming the position and responsibilities of a general even if he does have the ability. Probably, there should be more persons ordained to leadership in a day in which such persons seem to be in abundance in God's church. But laymen, on the other hand, must not be impatient for this since it is required of the present leadership that they not "lay hands" on people (ordain) too soon. Proper attitudes of humility, and willingness to become involved in the lowly aspects of the work of Christ, will eliminate most of the difficulties that grow out of this circumstance.

Thirdly, Paul writes: "Do not be wise in your own estimation"; that is where many persons in the lay movements of our time have erred. Because others did not see things their way, or did not do as they suggested, they launched out on their own in competition with the church or its leadership. This is the problem, for example, with counselors who hang out shingles and set themselves up as Christian counselors rather than work as pastor-teachers or elders under the aegis and authority of the Church of Christ. True, the church has not always been what it should be, and often has been slow to recognize and support the movements initiated by the Spirit of God, but setting up apart from and over against Christ's church solves nothing; it only weakens her impact. Think of a group of soldiers within the army deserting and setting out to fight the enemy on their own. More often than not, they will be pulling the rug out from beneath the feet of soldiers in the army rather than complementing their efforts.

You must recognize others in the church. They can help you (you will need them) and you can help them (they will need you). You must not try to go it alone. You must listen to them (especially respecting the leadership of the officers who have the rule over you) and work with them. The sun doesn't rise and set on your opinions alone! You don't have all the answers. Of course, neither do they. But they have some, just as you do, and you must never forget it. "But they never listen to me," you protest. Well, perhaps not, but one reason could be that you don't listen to them. Are you "wise in your own conceits"? Start listening more and you are likely to discover that you are beginning to be listened to.

There are Christians whose marriages have been suffering for years, who are unable to solve many problems on their own, who are truly perplexed over many issues who never get relief because of pride. This is another form of being wise in one's own eyes. "I'm a mess, but so is everyone else; nobody has any better answers than mine" expresses the attitude behind this failure to seek help. Blinded by his pride, a Christian can really convince himself that this is true. Of course, it isn't. There are many pastors and Christian brothers and sisters who could help you, were you to seek it. Eye, you need the foot; hand, you need the ear. Never forget it! The soldiers in an army are interdependent. Only someone blinded by pride could think otherwise. Confess your pride to God; seek forgiveness for it and go find help from your pastor, if you need it. Don't wait another day. You will never be able to overcome evil in another until you have learned to overcome it in yourself.

CHAPTER 12

No Exceptions Allowed

YES, THAT'S THE FACT. When you read verse 17 you immediately become aware of the fact that no exceptions are allowed: "*Never pay* back evil for evil to *anyone*." That part of the sentence contains an absolute ("never") that stands out as such because it can't be qualified ("never . . . to *anyone*").

The same reason why absolutes are unpleasant for some is why they are welcomed by others: they are unyielding in structure. Absolutes permit no exceptions. Because of this they are rare. Usually, commands refer to all of a group, a category, etc. Absolutes do not. Here we have one of two absolutes that occur in this chapter (the other is in verse 19: "*never* take your own revenge"). Absolutes are of particular importance because of their usefulness; there is never need to determine when a rule applies. If it is an absolute, it always applies.

You are bound to observe it with every person that you will ever come into relationship with. There will *never* be a time, a situation, or a person who is exempted. Never means never. You may *never* pay back evil for evil to anyone.

Absolutes help; they keep down confusion. They are very clear. If you can only accept it, an absolute is a great blessing. It fits all circumstances. No rationalizing is possible. You will never run into a situation when you'll have to puzzle out what to do. All you have to do is say, "OK, I'll have to live with this absolute"; then do so. Now, let's set the scene for considering this command.

In this book, we have been trying to discover how to overcome evil. The guiding principle we learned was that God expects us to overcome evil with good. We must bless—not curse—those who curse and otherwise persecute us. Our natural tendency (with which we were born as sinners) was to do the opposite, and even as believers we are still sinfully habituated to respond to evil with evil. Yet, the natural tendency and the habituated response may (must) be overcome by replacing it through the disciplined practice of biblical alternatives by the Spirit's renewing power. One way we can begin to exercise this corrective discipline is to accept the help and counsel of other members of the Lord's army. We must recognize that we cannot fight alone and win our battles with evil. There is need for a joint effort.

Some Christians fight at the drop of a hat. They snap back like an angry dog whose tail you've stepped on; they snarl and nip you in the leg. The verse we are looking at forbids such attitudes and actions: "*Never* pay back evil for evil." In other words you may not retaliate. You may not pay back in kind. You may not try to *get even* (note the words *pay back.*)

There is a perverted sense of righteousness that says "I'll even up the score," or "I'll get even." But God didn't give you that right. *He* evens up scores. You have neither the right nor ability to do so. (We'll come back to that when we study verse 19.) He has specifically forbidden you even to try to do so.

"But," you protest, "isn't there *some* time when I can do so? Isn't there *some* situation in which it's proper? Can't I *ever* give him back what he deserves?" NO; NEVER! This is never possible in personal relations.

Since childhood you've practiced the art of getting even ("Well, she pulled my hair first!"). This attitude is typical of children ("So much hair in her hands; so much hair in mine"), but it doesn't stop with them. In adults it simply becomes more subtle. This may be the ethic of business, psychology, science, or the guy down the street. And you may want your handful of hair too. But, Christian, it is not yours to have.

We have all done that sort of thing. Indeed, sometimes we've even spent inordinate amounts of time and effort planning how to pay back evil for evil. Some people go to great lengths to do this. I once heard of a man who paid alimony each month in nickels. He'd wheel it over to his former wife's house in a wheelbarrow and dump it out! Doubtless, this gave him a perverted sort of satisfaction. But think of the time and effort involved!

Yet "love doesn't retaliate" (1 Cor. 13:5c). And you must love your enemy by paying back so much *good* for so much evil. How are we ever going to begin to do this? How are we ever going to turn the corner? "I want to," you say, "but all my good resolutions go down the drain when the actual situation arises. How can I change?" The second part of verse 17 has the answer: "Respect what is right in the sight of all men."

First, let's translate that verse more accurately. (The word "respect" doesn't really convey the idea of the Greek original at all.) Here is how it should read: "Plan ahead" or "Make plans to do what is right in the sight of all men." In this clearer translation lies the key to the *how to do* what you are struggling with. If you want to overcome your own sinful tendencies and habits, you will have to make plans to do so. There is no other way. On the other hand, there is no better way. Most people fail because they do no such planning. Then they wonder why they fail.

Sinful tendencies and habits will prevail unless you have previously taken the time to plan (1) *what* (concretely) you will do and (2) *how* you will do it. It is difficult to overcome past patterns. Spur-of-the-moment, impulsive responses won't do. When you depend on impulse, habit takes over; and that is precisely what you want to overcome. Only deliberate planning for different responses, carefully spelled out in the cool rather than in the heat of the battle, is adequate. When you've been hit on the nose or kicked in the shins (literally or figuratively), pain and anger can cloud any but the most plain and deliberate plans.

Paul is against the emotionally oriented response because he knows it will lead us in the wrong direction. Instead, he tells you to take the time and make the effort to plan ahead like the general who, behind the lines of battle, lays his plans determining his countermoves *before* the enemy strikes. ("If he comes through this pass, I'll station my troops here.") You too must never go to battle until you have determined what you will do when trouble comes.

Now, let me ask you—have you ever sat down for even an hour to make such plans? Shouldn't you? Suppose someone cheats you in business, do you know how you should respond? Ever thought about it? Shouldn't you? Suppose somebody gossips about you. What are you going to do about that? Do you know how to handle it? Shouldn't you?

Take time to sit down and plan. Perhaps this is the operative key to the whole passage. How? First, ask what are the situations that I am most likely to face this next week that I have failed to meet successfully in the past. Write them out in the space below.

Situations I am likely to meet:

(Continued from previous page)

Secondly, work out your responses:

Good responses (planned ahead)[1]

---

1. Write these out in pencil. You will want to improve on them after reading more about how to do so later on.

Take time to talk over your responses with others (husband, wife, parent, pastor) who may be able to assist you. At first, good ideas may not come readily. Don't hesitate to work and rework your plans. Good plans take time and effort.[2] (After all, we often expend much time and effort in planning evil—remember the man with the wheelbarrow of nickels.)

Thirdly, be sure that every decision is made on the basis of biblical principle. If you can't think of a principle behind each plan, scrap it and work on another. Settle for nothing that doesn't clearly grow out of biblical principle. Keep working till that is certain. You don't want to exchange one bad habit for another. I shall say more about one critical principle that should apply in every case when I get to verse 20, but for now, begin to work on planning.

---

2. Planning means consideration and reconsideration of various possibilities until the best solutions are reached. Christians study the scriptural principles prayerfully until they are sure that they understand which ones apply to their situation. Then, they think of concrete applications to the situation itself.

CHAPTER 13

Plan with Finesse

MANY CHRISTIANS don't want to take the time and effort to do the planning that Paul commands. They would rather follow some ecstatic experience or some "leading" about how to act.[1] Right here is where the difference comes. There is no easy or quick path to holiness or to change. The Spirit of God did not take hundreds of years to produce a book by which to change and renew regenerate people only to ignore it and zap them at 2:30 Thursday morning! The only way to change is to study, believe, follow, and persist in biblical truth.

1. The word "led" occurs only twice in reference to the Spirit (in Rom. 8:14 and Gal. 5:18). Neither passage has to do with guidance. No information is given. In both places Paul is speaking about the Spirit leading (or empowering) the Christian to walk in the paths of righteousness. These ways, of course, are found in God's Word. "Leading," as so frequently used by Christians to denote feelings that impel one to make one choice or another, is an unscriptural concept.

Feelings and experiences may go back to nothing more than sleeplessness, unfortunate combinations of pickles, bananas, and ketchup, the weather, etc. But people want the instant experience rather than the hard work of planning. This passage warns against emotional responses to evil. Those who are wrapped up in them will have a difficult time with this admonition, but they must bring themselves to submit to it nonetheless. It is easy for none of us, because it means work. But, when we are willing to follow His Word, He both motivates and helps (cf. Phil. 2:13).

Paul says to plan ahead, but he doesn't tell you specifically what to do. You may be thinking, "I don't know what to do. Where do I begin?" If you don't know what to do, you must take time and make the effort to discover what to do; prayerfully study the Scriptures and think. Think with pen and paper. Planning requires the exercise of your mind; you cannot act on emotion alone. Most who return evil for evil are prone to act on emotion. This habit must be overcome. It will not be easy at first; it takes creativity to plan well. You will have to do some hard brain work. There is no list of things to do in the Bible, but you will probably have to make such a list before you are through. The general principles of the Scriptures must be translated into the concrete plans that fit each particular circumstance.

Think about those who have wronged you (who they are, what they are like) and are likely to do so again. Think of how it happened. Think then of what God wants you to do instead of what you did. (You may have to go back and seek forgiveness for past sinful responses if you haven't done so already.)

How long will planning take? More time at first; but it will be time well spent. The working out of the plan (once reached) also may take time. That man with the nickels must have given a great deal of time to coming up with that idea. It took him a lot of time each month preparing for the delivery too. I'd say he probably spent well over five hours a month just on that. Have you spent five minutes thinking about your responses to evil?

In 1 Thessalonians 5:15 we are commanded to "Seek after (the same word means "persecute") what is good for one another and for all men." Here, the idea of hard, diligent effort again comes to the fore. Seeking takes effort: You must *work at, pursue, track down the answer like a hound*. You may need to go over and over your plans, role playing what you will do and how you will do it, getting counsel and advice, etc. To do a good job takes time and effort. Love always involves such giving.

But there is one more important factor in this verse: "Plan *what is right* in the sight of everyone." Literally the Greek word means, "what is *fine* or *beautiful*."

You are to plan ahead. But you are to do more than that; you must plan to act with finesse. The plans that you lay must be so well thought through, so skillfully practiced (at least gone over in your mind), and so universally acknowledged as good that almost anyone would agree that what you did was *fine*. You must plan well and the plan must be well executed. The goodness of a deed, done in the wrong spirit or even done clumsily, can be nullified thereby.

Be sure too that *what* you do and *how* you plan to do it would receive universal approval. It should be done with all the universal qualities that would be looked for in a *Reader's Digest* article! So to do things well, you must plan ahead—and take time to let your plan mature so that you can give it that extra touch. The party, the dinner, the meeting, the wedding, and the Christian response that is done well were planned well in advance. We do few things well—even when we do the right thing—when we do them off the cuff.

"But am I to make men my standard?" you ask.
What do you mean?

"Paul says 'plan to do what is right *in every-one's sight*.' That sounds like seeking the approval of men."

Well, there is a great difference between making men your standard of what is fine and doing what God says is fine *in such a way that even unbelievers are forced to acknowledge that it was well done*. It is the latter that Paul has in view. He is concerned here about the *effect* of your response on others. He does not tell you to make your response one that is built on human standards. He wants to avoid the shoddy attempts that Christians make at doing good. He says our responses ought to be noteworthy. But your only standard for determining the response is the Bible.

So, take out your pencil and paper and your Bible and concordance[2] and go to work. Don't stop until you have a list of responses (what to do *and* how to do it) that you are enthusiastic about, and that you are sure others will recognize

---

2. If you don't know how to use Bible aids like concordances, commentaries, Bible dictionaries, and encyclopedias in Bible study then ask your pastor to give you some instruction in their use. Perhaps he would like to hold an eight- or ten-week class for you and some others.

as fine. Then—and only then—will you know so well what to do and how to do it that when the battle comes your new responses will issue naturally instead of the sinful ones that you have relied on before. Plan to pay back good for evil— with finesse!

CHAPTER 14

Make War, Make Peace

"IF POSSIBLE, so far as it depends upon you, be at peace with everybody" (Rom. 12:18). That is the next item on your list of battle orders.

You are required to defeat evil on the field of battle. But remember, winning the battle and achieving the peace are two distinct things. To win the war is only part of your orders; you are commanded as well to win the peace (if possible).

The parenthetical words in the last sentence introduce a note of stark realism into this command. There is no absolute here. Paul is totally realistic about the fact that, no matter how hard you try, you may fail in this endeavor. The reason why he is absolute about one order and conditional about another is because of the two different responsibilities involved. What you are responsible for he *requires*. When you are only halfway responsible, he requires you to assume only your half of the responsibility. There is no way that you can assume another person's responsibility for him; there is no way that you can make him be at peace with you if he doesn't want to be. I am glad that Paul was totally realistic about this. He is more reasonable than some Christians who wish to codify and neatly package everything. Some things simply don't wrap well in a sinful world.

You can always win the battle with evil—that depends on you. You can always win an inner peace—that also depends on you. But you can't always have peace with your defeated enemy.

Peace is your goal. The defeat of the enemy is not enough. You must look beyond this to the peaceful relations that you must try to establish once the enemy has surrendered. Sometimes—perhaps more often than you realize—this is possible (Yes, even with *your* in-laws!). If the focus is on the enemy rather than on yourself, if your concern is for him rather than to gloat over your victory, you will be more likely to do so. When Germany and Japan were defeated, they were also transformed into friends of the USA. But this happened only because extensive efforts were made to bring it about. Similarly, peace will not come automatically for you. As Hebrews 12:14 insists, you must "pursue" peace always.[1] It is always your goal, and you must strive for it in earnest.

Two things, then, are certain. If you don't realize that beyond the battlefield and the armistice table comes winning the peace, you will not seek it. So you *must* clearly set this goal from the outset and relentlessly pursue it throughout. Indeed, it will condition even the way that you conduct the war. You will be careful to see that no unnecessary destruction takes place. Secondly, you will be dissatisfied with winning alone. Unless your enemy can be turned from Satan and his crowd and won to faith in Jesus Christ, there can be no lasting peace at a level of depth. There can be partial, temporary peace, but nothing like the peace that comes from turning former enemies into allies. That is one of the reasons, like Christ and like Stephen, why you must pray for (bless) your enemy rather than curse him. You must seek peace of this sort at all (biblical) costs.

Some Christians don't believe that peace is always desirable. They think that if they aren't stirring up some conflict with the enemy they have become "unspiritual," or have "gone soft on the issues," or have "compromised." Yet that isn't the

1. Again the word for "persecuting" is used. Relentlessly pursuing peace until found—if at all possible—is the idea.

way the Scriptures put it. An elder, for instance, must have "a good reputation with those outside the church" (1 Tim. 3:7). If that is a requirement for a leader of the army—who is to be an example to those under him—it is likewise an ideal for the rest to attain.

Clearly, then, this passage assigns to the Christian soldier not only the task of successfully waging war; he is to be a *peacemaker* as well. Jesus' words "blessed are the peacemakers" apply here.

This verse also clears up many problems in counseling. Primarily, it has in view the relationship of a believer to unbelievers ("all men"). There is *always* a way to bring about peace with other believers through the reconciliation/discipline dynamic exercised by the church of Christ (Matt. 18:15ff.[2]). But since the church has no disciplinary jurisdiction over unbelievers, the same certainty does not exist in relationships with them. That is why Paul must say "so far as it [making peace] depends upon you." In every biblical way you are to try to make peace. You must do everything you can from your side of the relationship to bring it off.

Perhaps your unsaved mother-in-law isn't easy to get along with. That doesn't matter. You are a

2. For greater detail, see my chapter on this in *The Christian Counselor's Manual.*

Christian, and you have orders from your Commander in Chief: make peace with her if at all possible. You have no choice, no options, you must try to do so. You are to pursue those things that lead to peace *no matter what she does or says*. Your actions are to be the direct result of Christ's orders; they are not to be *re*actions to what she says or does. The Christian is free from all other human beings. He does not have to live over against others, controlled by their actions and responses. Rather, he lives according to Christ's commands. This is Christian freedom. It is a freedom unknown by others. It is not just when others do the things that we like that we act properly toward them; we are free to do good even when they don't because our actions are not dependent on their responses. It is the Lord Christ whom we serve! (cf. Matt. 5:44–48; Col. 3:22–25). That is what Paul means when he says "so far as it depends on you." Whether the other person pursues peace with you or not, then, is in one sense quite irrelevant. Your task, regardless of his response, is to do all that you ought to seek peace with him.

No matter what the other person does, if you know that you have done all that God requires you to do you can have an *inner* peace of your own from knowing you have done those things that please God. So, if pleasing God is your ultimate and prime goal, there is never really any time when you need to fail. Of course you may not reach peace with your enemy, but if you know that there is nothing more you could or should do from your side of the relationship, you know that you have succeeded: You have honored and pleased God.[3]

Now, the words "if possible" also limit the ways and means that you may use to bring about peace. The words "peace at any price" don't square with this important qualification. "If possible" indicates that there may be times when the cost of peace is too high. Peace must always be sought on a scriptural basis, with no compromise of biblical principle.

You see, peace is always possible. You can buy it at the cost of conscience, by compromising your beliefs or Christian behavior, etc. So there will be times when you must turn down the terms offered. You cannot sacrifice truth or holiness. You must seek peace through righteousness, never at the cost of righteousness.

There are three sides to every relationship: What another does, what you do, and what God does. Remember, then, you are not in this relationship

---

3. Cf. 2 Cor. 4:1–2, where Paul speaks in a similar vein.

alone. When you and God are in harmony, you constitute quite a majority (certainly more than 2^4 to 1) against your enemy! With this advantage, why should you cringe, whimper, whine, and despair? The advantage is all on your side. Even if he won't make peace on God's terms now by faith, ultimately he will do so by force.

But there are times when every effort has been made, that it is impossible to reach a peaceful settlement within a relationship, and the only recourse is to separate (cf. 1 Cor. 7:15). Even this, as the later part of 1 Corinthians 7:15 makes clear, should be done in the interest of peace. But peace *in* the relationship must always be the ideal for which you work.

"So far as it depends on *you*" is an important phrase because it indicates that Paul saw the importance of sorting out the responsibilities. Since the garden of Eden, where blame-shifting began ("The *woman* that *You* gave me, *she* . . ."; "the *snake*, *he!!!*"), sinners (even redeemed ones) have been confusing responsibilities. Paul's word is a clarion call for assuming responsibility. It is your responsibility before God to do all you can to bring about peace, *regardless of how the other party responds.*

4. Multiply this figure by infinity!

Now what are your responsibilities?

First, you must be right before God. Be sure that on all fronts you are at peace with Him first! Proverbs 16:7 says that "when a man's ways please God, He makes even his enemies to be at peace with him." The book of Judges clearly points out how God often uses enemies to bring His people to repentance and fellowship with Him. It could be that the basic battle must be fought inside you with your own sin. Check out *all* your relationships (not only those with your enemy). When you are right with your spouse, your parents, your employer, your neighbor, your children, etc., often God will melt the enemy's hostilities before you.

But, secondly, the presence of an enemy may not be correctional (cf. Heb. 11). It may be that God wants you to win him to Christ; it may be that He wants you to triumph over him for His name's sake as a witness, or to stretch and strengthen you to help you to grow—who knows? So your second responsibility is to be right before your enemy. If there is sin you must confess, or wrongs you must right with him, then don't hesitate or delay. As embarrassing, as difficult as it may be, go ahead immediately and make matters right.

"Won't it be a bad testimony to him to admit I wronged him?" No, he already knows that. As a

Christian you don't profess to be perfect. Rather, you profess to be a sinner saved by grace. Saved, yes; perfect yet, no. You are only *affirming* your belief when you confess and right a wrong with another. It is difficult, but not nearly so difficult as carrying the load of unforgiven guilt and stress before God and your neighbor.

Be a peacemaker; begin today!

CHAPTER 15

Three Ways to Be a Troublemaker

SO, YOU—A SOLDIER of the cross—are to be a peacemaker too! Well, then, why aren't you making peace more than you do? Why are you such a troublemaker instead? Perhaps the answer to this is found in three ways you can cause problems. Paul was in many scraps as an apostle, but he could never be charged with starting them.

Yet, that is the first way in which Christians can become troublemakers rather than peacemakers: *they can provoke trouble*. In 2 Thessalonians 3:12 we are urged instead to live a *quiet* life. We are to work and conduct our affairs in a quiet manner. We are never to pick fights. As a promoter of peace, you are not to ask for trouble, but rather to do all you can to see to it that trouble doesn't get started in the first place. It is not enough to know how to bring about peace by ending hostilities; we must promote peace instead of war. When war comes, the Christian must fight and fight to win. But he is never, by his own sin, to trigger an explosion.

We often read about great servants of God who find themselves "on the firing line." They are often on the firing line, it is true, but if they are truly serving Christ, it is His message and truth that put them there—not their own feisty attitudes or approaches. God has called you to peace; you may not fire the first shot! If you are busy serving Christ, you won't have either the time or the inclination to pick fights. As a matter of fact, if you serve Him faithfully, you'll have little need to pick fights. Your hands will be full dealing with the enemies who are attacking you. God's true servants deplore the fact that they must build with a trowel in one hand and a sword in the other. They would far rather use both hands building! But if challenged by attacks from the evil one, they can and will fight (with good) and win!

Secondly, troublemakers not only provoke trouble, they also are past masters at *protracting trouble*. Indeed, they may not provoke trouble at all; but whenever troubles come they are right there at the front egging it on instead of pacifying. In contrast, Paul says that "when slandered," he tried to "conciliate" (1 Cor. 4:13). That is a spirit quite foreign to the troublemaker. The troublemaker, in contrast, welcomes trouble. He looks for trouble. He knows how to find a spark of trouble and fan it into a flame. Instead of quieting trouble, he widens and deepens it. In short, he protracts or extends trouble by getting others involved, introducing new elements, etc. His attitude is, "I didn't start this, but I'm sure ready for it!" He has a zest for battle, whereas the peacemaker is ready too but he regrets the necessity to fight.

The elder must not be a striker or quick tempered (Titus 1:7). He must be a peacemaker. Neither should any Christian be a troublemaker; the elder sets the example for the flock in all things (Titus 2:7).

The Scriptures teach that you must narrow rather than broaden the scope of conflict. "A soft answer turns away wrath" (Prov. 15:1). Harsh words stir up more strife, but a soft reply narrows, confines, and abates it. The troublemaker gives a harsh reply; the peacemaker has planned to speak soft words and knows how to do so.

When you play ping-pong you know how this works. Someone smashes the ball toward you. You move away from the table to receive it. If you smash it back in return, he too moves farther away. The gap between you widens as the ball gets smashed from one side of the table to the other. But if you return a soft answer to his smash—one that barely clears the net—you pull him in closer to you and narrow the gap between the two of you. Soft answers bring people together; they bring peace. Hard answers drive them farther apart.

Doubtless you are familiar with the old stage routine: One man comes out whispering. His friend, whispering too, answers him. They go on talking back and forth this way for some time when the second man says, "Say, Joe, what are we whispering for?" Joe replies, "I don't know about you, but I've got laryngitis." A soft answer is imitated (as indeed, experiments have shown, a loud one is too).

In every way, then, the peacemaking child of God must endeavor to constrict rather than protract trouble as he promotes peace.

Thirdly, a troublemaker *prolongs trouble*. According to Ephesians 4:26, a Christian must never go to bed angry; matters are to be settled that day. They may not be carried over to the next day. In Matthew 5:18 Jesus makes it clear by the word of priority that He uses ("first") that getting matters settled between squabbling believers takes precedence even over worship itself. It is an item of the highest priority. Worship must be interrupted to see to it. There is a note of urgency in this, as also there is in a similar passage in Matthew 5:25 (note the word "quickly").

But the troublemaker finds excuses for prolonging a conflict rather than bringing it to an end as quickly as possible: "My temperament clashes with someone like that," or "Oh, it's no use trying to make peace with him, I've tried it before and I know what he'll say," or "I just don't know what to say if I do go," etc. Quickly, let's just take up those three common objections. First, "Our temperaments clash." This verse says to be at peace with "*all* men." That includes all sorts and conditions of men; all classes, all *temperaments*. The matter of temperaments is irrelevant. Your task is to see to it that *your* temperament is under control so that you don't mindlessly clash with him.

Secondly, "It's no use; I've tried it before." Christians who speak that way (and many do, unfortunately) deny God's power to change people. Theoretically, they accept this possibility, but their words and actions belie their professed beliefs. The Christian, in love, never gives up ("love never fails"). That means he keeps on "hoping all things." He knows that (perhaps in answer to his own prayers) no matter how often Bill has responded in one way in the past, God may have done something between the last time and this to change Bill. How often have I seen this happen in counseling! It is unloving for one person to prejudge the response of another, and it virtually denies the value of the prayer that one makes requesting just such a change. Love and faith characterize the peacemaker just as suspicion and doubt characterize the troublemaker.

Thirdly, there are those who protest that they don't know how to approach another to seek peace. This excuse has a certain amount of plausibility, and he can even convince himself that it is true. People don't know how to face unpleasant problems. But that doesn't mean they can't learn. And in the light of the urgency that the Scriptures enjoin on us to get matters settled right off, it is obviously a high priority item to learn how. One can always ask his pastor for help! Ironically, it is usually *easier* to settle matters quickly, before they become needlessly complicated or harden into bitterness and resentment.

One way to approach another, when you can't come up with a better one, is to say, "I've got a problem. (*You do*: how to approach him.) There is something I've got to say to you and I want to say it well, but I haven't been able to figure out how best to. So I'm simply going to tell you." Then drop it. This takes the edge off the situation, lets the other fellow know of your good intentions and concern for doing this well, and gets you right to the heart of the issue. It isn't the best way; but when you have no better way, it will do.

You may not win the peace after every battle, nor always prevent war from breaking out, but those are the two objectives that God has given you when He said "be at peace with all men."

CHAPTER 16

Christian Vigilantes?

THE GENERAL guiding principle that covers all Paul has written in this section is, "Do not be overcome by evil, but overcome evil with good." This is the battle order Christ issued to His church. You are to win your battles against evil. We have been trying to see how God expects us to do that. We've talked about many of the specific details behind those orders that appear in verses 14–18. Now we come to verse 19. This verse clarifies a perplexing aspect of the program by adding a very crucial element to it: We do not have to fight this war alone, not even together with the rest of the army. There are aspects of the war that will be handled by the Commander in Chief Himself.

Had you not been told this, you might have supposed that the war depended solely on you and others like you. You know your orders; but you

123

know that you often forget them. You know your orders; but you have trouble following them. And you know that others in the army are not always dependable either. Thankfully, the wise Commander has kept for Himself the ultimate issue of all things, and those aspects of the war that you and I never could have handled anyway.[1] This is a great encouragement.

Verse 19 reads: "*Never* take your own revenge, beloved, but leave room for wrath. It is written, 'Vengeance is Mine; I will repay, says the Lord.'"

We have discovered that a Christian's attitude and his actions are to be good. Good actions, based on an understanding of the Scriptures and a desire to please God by obedience to them, will lead to good attitudes.[2] Focusing on the person who has wronged you—his needs and problems—rather than yourself (for instance) will help avoid self-pity and will lead to a better attitude for witnessing to him and winning him. Planning ahead is another action that can have a lot to do with the attitude that one has when he finds himself engaged in

1. Of course, He is working also even through our sins and failures to bring about His sovereign purposes. Seeming setbacks, part of His plan, ultimately will only further His aims. That, however, by no means removes the responsibility of every soldier to fight well.

2. See my *Christian Counselor's Manual* for more information on attitudes.

hand-to-hand combat with evil on the field of battle. All this we have seen and, because we have these foundational truths fixed in mind, it is possible to go on.

Verse 19 teaches additional truth that is critical to waging war successfully. It says, in effect, that your actions and attitudes will be influenced by your understanding and acceptance of the biblical limitations placed on your authority and ability as an individual soldier in the Lord's army. In meeting evil with good, you have a limited, circumscribed, and clearly defined sphere of activity that you may not go beyond. When you do, you give aid to the enemy, usurp the authority that has been reserved for Another, and endanger yourself in the bargain.

In setting forth these limitations, the apostle used his second absolute: "*Never* take your own revenge." It is really a reiteration of the one previously given in verse 17, "*Never* pay back evil for evil," with a slightly different emphasis, to which an important reason and promise is appended: "Vengeance is Mine"; "I will repay." When Paul says never, he means just that. There is *never* a time when the Christian—as an individual—on his own authority may take vengeance on another. There are no special circumstances. The rule admits of no qualifications.

"But no one else seems to be doing anything about it; if I don't, he'll get away with what he did!" The objection is invalid. God has said He will take care of the matter in His time and His way. There are no exceptions to the rule. God's surveillance of the situation is complete; He misses nothing. There will be no failures in His justice. Your impatience, in view of this verse, is really impertinence! Hands off. Vengeance does not belong to you!

"But, I can do it so easily. I'm in a perfect position as his boss to do so. I could right all the wrongs and everyone would be happier. Perhaps, in the long run, he would be too." No exceptions. You are *never* in the right position to execute justice as a private person. God has reserved that position for Himself. Step aside; you are standing where you have no right to be.

"Why?"

There are fundamentally two answers to that question:

1. God hasn't given you the *authority* (right) to take vengeance.
2. God hasn't given you the *ability* to take vengeance.

Let's consider those two reasons carefully. First, as He says so plainly ("Vengeance is Mine"), vengeance belongs to Him. You—as an individual—have no right to take vengeance; He has allocated that right to Himself alone. Whenever you do so, wittingly or unwittingly (as is usually the case), you attempt to arrogate a prerogative that belongs to God. That is, in plain unvarnished English, stealing. The man or woman who takes vengeance usurps the authority God has reserved for Himself. Vengeance is *not your job!* It is His.

Christians who take vengeance into their own hands strap on the six-guns, coil up their ropes, and ride off into the sunset as truly as did the vigilantes on the frontier. You are a lawless person when you do so; you are taking the law—God's law (mind you)—into your own hands! You are as guilty before God as the person on whom you seek to take vengeance. Vengeance is never "sweet" (as the saying has it) because it is a rebellious act, perpetrated in the full face of clear Scripture that forbids it!

Look down at your side, Christian. See those holsters and guns? Loosen that belt, untie the cord around your right leg, let the guns fall off as you sink to your knees before your God in repentance, confessing your sin and seeking His fatherly forgiveness. Your Wild West days are over. You may have been a gunslinger before you came to know Christ; you have now been inducted into the army of the Lord. Go ahead, strip those guns from your side. You have taken an oath to follow Him and serve him *His* way. He forbids vigilantism. You may *never* engage in such lawless activities; *never*. Get that straight, once and for all!

What is vengeance? This verse parallels it with wrath. Together, the two concepts seem to indicate that vengeance is repaying someone for his evil deeds in wrath. It is more than just retaliation (striking back). There is a planned, deliberate, calculated aspect to it. But your task is to plan to do good; you are never instructed to plan to execute wrath.

Vengeance is also a judicial thing as the Greek term used for vengeance indicates. This is important because it leads us to the fact that vengeance is limited to those who have the authority to execute justice. God, of course, is the One in Whom all such authority resides ultimately. And *ultimately*, He is the One Who will judge and right all wrongs (in His Son, Jesus Christ). However, to a small degree, He delegates aspects of His vengeance to the rightful authorities in the state and the church. It is interesting how the conjunction of subjects in chapters 12 and 13 of Romans makes clear the critical distinction between the authority of the individual, whose personal ethic from God forbids all vengeance taking, and the authority of the civil ruler, who is given authority from God (13:1) to be "an avenger who brings wrath upon the one who practices evil." That distinction must always be kept in mind: the Christian—as a private person—never may take revenge; the Christian—as a civil magistrate—has the authority and obligation to do so.

In this day in which civil magistrates either imperfectly assume their obligation (or rarely do so at all) I am tempted to discuss this failure and the devastating effects it has had on our culture. But I dare not. This is not a book on civil ethics, but deals with personal ethics alone.

I would like also to say more about the importance of church officers (the elders of the church ordained to exercise rule and discipline) assuming their authority to "bind and loose." Since I have said something about this in the *Manual* (and elsewhere), and because I am sketching out a book on church discipline at the present time, I will say only a bit here.

The officers of the church are to judge *outward* actions (only God judges the heart[3]). They

---

3. 1 Sam. 16:7: "Man looks on the outward appearance; God looks on the heart." That is one reason why Gene Getz's horrendous suggestion that "mental adultery" is an adequate ground for divorce is decidedly unscriptural (Gene A Getz, *The Measure of a Family* (G/L Publications, Glendale: 1976), 169.

excommunicate only on the basis of persistent refusal to hear exhortation from other Christians and themselves assembled officially as the representatives of Christ's church (cf. Matt. 18:15–20). It is hard enough for the civil magistrate and for the leaders of the visible church to exercise justice concerning overt behavior based on actual observable transgressions (of course, they fail miserably; that is why God alone is the Judge and ultimate Avenger Who will right all wrongs).

It is wrong for individual Christians to excommunicate other professed Christians in their hearts. No Christian can judge another in the church to be an unbeliever; that is the task of the church officers, acting as such! He has not been given that right. Instead, he is to believe and hope all things in love. On the other hand, church officers must begin to exercise proper discipline over the flock. The blessings of care and discipline are privileges that belong to the members of God's flock and should not be withheld from them. It is the right of every member of Christ's church to be confronted informally by any member of the church when he sins overtly (Gal. 6:1; Matt. 18:15f.) and to be judged formally by the church officers if he doesn't heed informal overtures. A professed member is declared to be "as a heathen and a publican," however, only by the officers acting in excommunication or when he himself apostatizes from the church (1 John 2:19). Only then—when the party is no longer under the care and discipline of the church—may the individual Christian treat him as an unbeliever. If the church officers are not exercising discipline as they should, individual Christians must use their influence to see to it that this situation is quickly corrected. But nonetheless, God has given you, as an individual Christian, no right to judge in your heart that other professed believers are really non-Christians. That too is a form of vigilantism, *within the church*, that Christ will not tolerate.

"But our church has no discipline!" Perhaps that is so. Nevertheless, two wrongs, two violations of God's Word, don't make it right. The vigilante is one who always gets a following *because* law and order are relaxed. Otherwise he wouldn't get a hearing. The answer to the problem *at every level* is not to take the law into one's own hands, but to lend all one's efforts toward restoring proper law and order. And if it takes time and people seem to be getting away with murder, don't fret—God will repay. He promises. No one gets away with anything.

He knows and judges all. Leave it to Him to adjust the scales that seem so unbalanced. That job belongs to Him. James 4:11–12 is a verse for every individual (as such): "Do not speak against one another, brethren. He who speaks against a brother or judges his brother, speaks against the law and judges the law [he doesn't like the restrictions God has placed on him in His law; he wants to be judge himself]; but if you judge the law you are not a doer of the law but a judge of it [you think you are *above* God's law when you criticize or disobey the limitations it places on you]. There is only one Lawgiver and Judge [you have neither God's authority nor ability], the One who is able to save and to destroy [you can't do this; but what kind of lawgiver or judge would you be unless you could enforce and uphold a law that you gave?]; but who are you [weak, impotent creature that you are] who judges your neighbor?"

A vigilante, then, is one who with neither the right nor the power to do so, takes the law into his own hands. What he doesn't do—note this well—is give that alleged offender the right to a fair trial. God does so because God alone is *able* to do so. God ultimately will judge Hitler, Mary Baker Glover Patterson Eddy, your enemies, etc.

God is no vigilante. All the facts will be aired; the evidence will be examined; justice will be shown. Every man will get his day in court. Nobody who goes to hell will have anything to complain about.

All of which leads to the second point. . . .

CHAPTER 17

Make Room for God!

GOD HAS NOT given you the ability to take vengeance on others.

You should be delighted that God has removed this onerous responsibility from you. You don't have to take on yourself the awesome responsibility of judging others and pronouncing the judgment on them that is fitting to their crimes. The responsibility is too great for you. You don't have the ability to do it; the job is too large for you! And most amazingly, God has said, "I'll take care of it Myself." The matter won't be swept under the rug or shelved and never raised again. "I'll get around to it in My time and in My way. Perhaps partly now, but fully on the day of judgment.[1] I know all that

---

1. Even all wrongs between believers will not be settled here (1 Thess. 4:6). In this passage Paul tells the Thessalonians (and you) that individual church members don't have the right to take vengeance. The Lord is the Avenger. Paul solemnly warned

has happened; I know what to do about it. I have the power to right all wrongs, and I have promised to do so." Well then Christian, why shove *your* oar in? What are you doing when you get involved in this vengeance business anyway? Leave it to God. He'll deal with it quite satisfactorily.

Love is your task. Vengeance is the opposite of love for one's neighbor. In Leviticus 19:18, the passage from which Christ took His second great commandment, loving one's neighbor is set over against taking vengeance on him. The two tasks are diametrically opposed. Your job is not to get even, take out your wrath, curse and damn another, but to overcome his evil with your good.

You are also instructed to "leave room for wrath," i.e., for God's wrath.[2] Vengeance doesn't belong to you. Wrath is God's business. So, if you are standing in the Judge's place—move! You're standing on holy ground. You have no right there!

---

them not to take things into their own hands. God will right all wrongs. Sometimes God uses church discipline now; sometimes He judges directly now (1 Cor. 11:29, 30), sometimes he waits till later.

2. The words "of god" are not in the original but are a correct interpretation. The idea here is not that you should give in to the enemy's wrath (that would be contradictory to all else said here). The spirit of the passage is active, not passive, as verses 10, 21 clearly indicate.

God wants to stand there—make room for Him and His wrath!

If you drive to work (or school) you may have noticed the president's parking space with its sign: RESERVED FOR THE PRESIDENT. If you know what's good for you, you will keep your car out of it. You won't park there. You'll *leave room* for the president!

God says, "I've reserved the business of vengeance for myself." So in this passage (as well as elsewhere) He posts His sign: KEEP OUT. "Make room for Me," He says thereby; "this is my parking place."

In the army, a soldier had better not try to take over the job of his superior. Neither may you take over the task that the Commander in Chief has reserved for Himself.

The pictures conjured up by God's insistent command "leave room" are almost endless. Each contributes something. I'll mention but two others. "Leave room. I'm coming through. Don't be in My way when I do." You can't stop God from parking, and He won't take another place: He'll park right through you! For your own good, get out of His way!

Finally, take the little child standing up to a bully towering head and shoulders over him. Then, his dad comes and says, "Step aside, son. I'll take care of him." Step aside for God.

All these things are bound up in this encouraging warning—"leave room for wrath."

It's something like the Greyhound Bus TV commercial that goes ". . . and, leave the driving to us." Leave the vengeance to God. You have to anyhow, because you don't really have the ability to take vengeance. He is the only One Who can do so. You are a finite, biased, involved sinner. How could you really right wrongs anyway? Come on now!

You don't even know what your enemy truly deserves. You don't know his heart, and your knowledge of the outward facts at best is always partial. You might give him too much wrath— or too little. Even the judgment that God has given to the state and to the church is incomplete because neither can judge motives (and the state and church are wrong whenever they try to do so). He is the only One Who can lay bare the inner man and know all his thoughts and intentions (Heb. 4:12, 13).

Recently, after I had delivered a lecture, a college professor raised an objection to what I had said while challenging the student body. "You have flattered these students," he charged. I was dumbfounded. He had judged beyond his facts. The last thing that had occurred to me was to flatter anyone. I was trying to encourage and challenge. Since that was the first time in my whole speaking career that I had ever been accused of flattery (usually I am accused of the opposite, if anything), I simply didn't know what to say (*I hadn't planned ahead* for that one!). I now know. I shall say simply (in the future), "Sir, you have sinned against me; you have judged my motives. God doesn't grant you that right. But I am prepared to forgive you if you repent."

Note the word "beloved," which means "My dear one." God wants you to know that He cares for you. He hasn't forgotten the wrongs done to you. You are dear to Him. He will right those wrongs. He knows what you have suffered, and He cares. He knows you would like to see justice done now. But He also knows what you don't—why it is better to wait. Remember those "souls under the altar" crying out for vengeance. They had to wait. They ask, "How long, Lord? How long?" He says, "A little while" (Rev. 6:9–11). They must wait till all the purposes of God are carried forth. But the day came when their time of waiting ended. So too will yours. God will right all wrongs because He cares for you.

The day is coming when He will come in flaming fire with His angels *taking vengeance* on those who do not know Him (2 Thess. 1:5–12), and He will turn the tables on those who now afflict you. But, it may well be that He is waiting for another purpose. He may be waiting for your witness in suffering to lead some of the enemy into His camp. Let's study the next verse and see.

CHAPTER 18

Meet Your Enemy's Need

WE COME NOW to verse 20, the final verse in this discussion to be considered. It was not only because I knew that you'd be intrigued with it that I saved it till last (I wonder how many of you turned to the discussion of this verse first), but in emphasis as well as in the natural order of the passage, it forms a fitting conclusion to the whole. Paul writes: "If your enemy is hungry feed him; if he is thirsty give him a drink. By doing so you will heap burning coals on his head."

Does this—heaping coals on an enemy's head—sound like love and doing good to him? Does it sound like blessing? Doesn't it sound (rather) like taking vengeance? Is this a contradiction to all that Paul has said elsewhere? Certainly not. I shall show you how the two fit hand-in-glove all in good time, but at the moment we must delay our discussion long enough to consider one or two other matters first.

What is an enemy? You must show love for an enemy by feeding him or giving him something to drink. But you must first understand what Paul is talking about. An enemy is not someone who does something evil to you once. This is an *extreme* statement. Casually dip into the psalms of David and notice what an enemy does. He sets traps for you, tries to take your life, spreads slander and gossip about you, waits to ambush you, etc. In other words, an enemy is somebody who has made it his full-time job to make you miserable or to put you out of the way. To do good to an *enemy*, then, is to do good to the hardest one of all. Yet Christ said "love your enemies" (Matt. 5:44). The depth of this concept is revealed in the 23rd Psalm where the supreme triumph of the eternal state is described as God preparing a table *in the presence of one's enemies*. In Romans 5, we are told that Christ died for the ungodly (v. 6). That is remarkable. But beyond that, He died for sinners (v. 8). That is even more remarkable. At the greatest extreme, Christ died for His enemies (v. 10). That is most remarkable of all. Christ died for those who hated Him, who (like Paul) were actively engaged in scattering (destroying God's work) rather than gathering (promoting it).

How do you do good to an enemy? Here, you are required to discover your enemy's need and meet it: "If he is hungry . . . if he is thirsty." The first thing you must do is discover a legitimate need in your enemy's life. In planning to do good to those who wrong you, this element must be added. In chapter 12, when you were planning good responses with which to meet evil I mentioned that further qualifications would be needed to adequately do the job. Turn back to that section, reread what you wrote in the blank spaces provided, and revise your answers in terms of this principle.

The important principle that one must keep in mind in returning good for evil is that the best response is one that meets a pressing need (here hunger and thirst represent, but do not exhaust, that general principle). In Titus 3:14 Paul writes, "Let our people also learn to engage in good deeds to meet pressing needs that they may not be unfruitful."[1]

Remember, you don't have to feel like it (that at times is entirely out of the question) to meet an enemy's needs. You do it—not because you have

1. See appendix to my volume *Coping with Counseling Crises* for an original song based on this verse.

whomped up a warm and benevolent feeling toward him, but because God tells you to, and you want to please God. You don't love by feeling; you love by feeding. Love begins with *giving* (cf. John 3:16; Gal. 2:20; Eph. 5:25). You must give whatever you have in order to meet his need, whatever it is.

So, planning of your responses to evil must include research of your enemy. You must find out his needs. That may take time and effort. You cannot simply guess about his needs. This also (once again) takes the focus off yourself, helps you to understand him better (perhaps even a bit more about what is behind his actions), and in the end, *at the very least*, puts you in a position to do some *significant* good for him.

After researching your enemy's needs, you must take an inventory of your own resources. Consider your funds (the least satisfactory solution in most cases), your ingenuity, your possessions, your thoughts, your time, your life (or any or all of these) and determine what you have that can meet (at least in part) his need. Then give it to him—with no strings attached. It should be a pure gift from which no return is expected (Luke 6:35). Be sure you plan ahead *exactly* how much, what items you will give, etc., leaving nothing in doubt. Uncertainty can lead to trouble.

Thirdly, look for the right opportunity (or make it) to meet his needs. Be sure that you don't create new problems by bad timing or the manner in which you seek to meet his need. The whole thing—remember—must be carried off from start to finish with finesse. So, the principle of meeting needs is fundamental to planning how to do good to another. Don't forget it; it is the key to what follows.

CHAPTER 19

Pour on the Coals

"BY DOING SO," Paul says, "you will heap burning coals on his head." This cannot mean taking vengeance on your enemy since Paul has just finished teaching the opposite in verse 19. Well, then, what does it mean?

Heaping coals on your enemy's head is intimately connected with meeting his needs. When you meet his needs, you pour on the coals. And thus, as the following verse makes clear, you overcome evil with good.

There is no thought of punishment here, or of pangs of conscience burning within him. Your goal is to overcome his evil with your good. *The coals are your good deeds heaped on him.*

Remember, Paul has warfare in mind. In his day they didn't have flame throwers, but they knew that fire was an effective weapon. If you could get coals (of smokeless undetectable charcoal, as the word here indicates) on your enemy's head, you would effectively put him out of business as an enemy. You would subdue and overcome him.

Picture your troops holding the heights above the pass. Secretly you have heated large beds of charcoal to white heat. As the unsuspecting enemy passes directly beneath, you shovel them off on his head. You have him! You've defeated him! He is rendered powerless, helpless! You've stopped him in his tracks. That is the picture.

If you do enough good, it will be like using napalm. Your good deeds will so blunt his attack, disorient and discourage him, that he'll be ineffective as an enemy.

Be sure, however, that you "heap" coals on his head. That is to say, be sure you do enough good to him. You cannot settle for a token effort. Enough also may mean enough *over a period of time*. (You may have to do it much more than once.) It may mean a large enough effort. But whatever you do should be more than adequate: good must be heaped on his head.

God Himself used this method on the cross. There He heaped up goodness beyond sufficiency in that sacrifice of infinite worth. Where sin abounded, grace far more abounded. God returned this good for our evil. Why? Romans 2:4 answers that question: "the kindness of God is to lead you to repentance." That's the very point. God gives good food and drink to His enemies in their need to win to His side those for whom Christ died.

When you have effectively enough put an enemy out of business as an enemy, by heaping good on him, he may surrender to Jesus Christ and be led in His triumphal parade as a trophy of His salvation (cf. 2 Cor. 2:14). Let your drink of water introduce your enemy to the Water of Life; share your bread so that your enemy may be attracted to the Bread of Life. The most effective way to defeat an enemy is to induce him to come over to your side.

When God sent His Son to die for guilty sinners—for His enemies—Jesus Christ became the greatest demonstration of this verse of all time. That it works is evident because that is why you and I are part of the King's army today.

CHAPTER 20

Epilog

ALL RIGHT NOW. You have studied the golden theme of Romans 12:14–21: Overcome evil with good. You know what that means concretely. Now it is time to act, if you have not done so already.

First, sit down and think about it; who are those who are doing evil things to you at the present time? Christians? Unbelievers? Enemies? Family? Neighbors? Business associates?

Then, ask yourself, "How have I responded?" Be candid. Don't gloss over the facts. Pray for wisdom to truly remember and evaluate honestly. Make a sober judgment about how you handled persecution and trouble.

Next, ask God's forgiveness for any wrongs uncovered. Plan also to seek forgiveness from those whom you wronged, at the earliest appropriate moment.

Also, begin planning how to respond in the future. Keep in mind that you may even be called on to make a new response when you go to seek forgiveness. So don't put off planning. Get to work on it right away. Continue to work on it in all sorts of dimensions for various situations and people for a good while to come.

When you plan, write out what you will do *in the light of the enemy's needs*. Study his needs and your resources, and determine how and when to bring the two together. (Don't put this off too long either. Get to it before further complications arise.)

Heap good on your enemy. When you plan your response be sure that you plan one that seems more than adequate. In that way it is unlikely that you will inadequately return good for evil (remember the word heap). Destroy his effectiveness; win the battle and try to win the man. Do what you plan to do with finesse. Plan details, practice *how* you will carry out your plan. Pray that God will bring him to repentance.

May God bless you and your enemies through you!